The Basilian Aphorisms

THE
BASILIAN APHORISMS

OR THE HERMETIC CANONS OF
THE SPIRIT, SOUL, AND BODY OF
THE MAJOR & MINOR WORLD

Collected by
HERMOPHILO PHILOCHEMICO

Edited, Translated, & Annotated by
Mirco A. Mannucci, PhD,
& Aaron Cheak, PhD

RUBEDO PRESS
AUCKLAND · 2018

RUBEDO PRESS

*The Basilian Aphorisms:
Or the Hermetic Canons of the Spirit, Soul,
and Body of the Major and Minor World*

Edited, Translated, and Annotated by

Mirco A. Mannucci &
Aaron Cheak

———

First published in 2018 by

RUBEDO PRESS
PO BOX 21266
AUCKLAND 0650
NEW ZEALAND

© Rubedo Press 2018

ISBN: 978-0-473-41371-2

All rights reserved.
No part of this work may be reproduced
without express permission from the publisher.
Brief passages may be cited by way of criticism,
scholarship, or review, as long as full
acknowledgement is given.

———

Design and Typography
by Aaron Cheak

SCRIBE SANGUINE QUIA SANGUIS SPIRITUS

TABLE OF CONTENTS

Acknowledgements
7

Preface
9

INTRODUCTION
Raphæl Eglinus Iconius
and the Basilian Aphorisms
13

TEXT AND TRANSLATION
Aphorismi Basiliani | *The Basilian Aphorisms*
30 | 31

ANNOTATIONS &
COMMENTARY
73

Bibliography
111

About the Contributors
117

Acknowledgements

THE PRINCIPAL TRANSLATOR WISHES, first and foremost, to thank Dr. Aaron Cheak for the great opportunity of publishing this work with Rubedo Press. Together with the *Hermetic Recreations*, it represents the emergence of a scintillating new series of potent alchemical classics intended to open Anglophone readers into the fascinating albeit nebulous world of traditional western alchemy.

Our deepest gratitude must also be given to our lifelong friend, Professor Riccardo Di Giuseppe, for kindly revising an earlier version of the translation, and to Michael A. Putman, for carefully reviewing the final translation. To the latter we are especially grateful for his careful assistance with some of the thornier passages that this text presents.

Finally, because this text is intended not only for scholars and students, but also for practitioners of the royal art, a heartfelt *grazie* must be extended to all the members of the discussion group, *Alchimia Reale*. In particular, we extend our thanks to three valiant operative alchemists working under the *noms de plume* of Flavio Claudio Giuliano (Marco Panciroli), Giovanni Atrop, and Fernando Durante, who provided important insights and references in their comments upon some of the canons.

MIRCO A. MANNUCCI

Preface

THE SMALL HERMETIC JEWEL THAT WE PRESENT HERE is distilled from the bewildering array of alchemical precepts and practices that proliferated in Mediæval and Early Modern Europe. Published in Marburg in 1608, it bears the distinct influence of two foundational figures of Early Modern alchemy: Theophrastus Bombastus von Hohenheim, *alias* Paracelsus (1493/4–1541), and Basilius Valentinus (attributed to the fifteenth century). From Paracelsus, the doctrine of the *tria prima* or three principles would take centre stage. This doctrine, together with Paracelsus' re-articulation of the macrocosm-microcosm homology, would prove decisive for subsequent alchemical theory in the west. Of Basilius Valentinus, it is enough to emphasise the pivotal motif of the metallic seed, which like a tree, grows through the seven phases of metallic transformation, and ripens into the fruits of silver and gold. Perhaps more important still is the vegetative metaphor that this theme employs, for it firmly places the so-called inanimate aspects of reality (i.e., minerals, metals) within the full purview of a living, vitalist worldview. Among the many fruits emerging from this confluence of Paracelsian and Valentinian ideas, the *Basilian Aphorisms* can be considered a genuine pith-teaching.

The *Aphorismi Basiliani* consist of eighteen 'Hermetic Canons' which cut to the heart of the triadic structure of the macrocosm and microcosm. Describing both the external world of nature, in which three kingdoms prevail, and the human trichotomy of spirit, soul, and body, the *Basilian Aphorisms* are designed for deep meditation upon the thrice-great Hermetic mystery: Sulphur, Mercury, and Salt.

Presented here in English for the very first time, this edition provides the original Latin text alongside a facing-page translation, followed by a concise commentary upon the significance of each canon. While the Introduction to this volume attempts to situate the work within its proper historical, biographical, and bibliographical contexts, the commentary and annotations that follow are not intended to provide an exhaustive scholarly analysis. Rather, they are meant to remain more hermeneutically open.

Mirco A. Mannucci
& Aaron Cheak

RAPHÆL EGLINUS ICONIUS
*Österreichische Nationalbibliothek
Bildarchiv und Grafiksammlung*

Introduction

RAPHÆL EGLINUS ICONIUS
AND THE BASILIAN APHORISMS

AT FIRST GLANCE, this short collection of Hermetic aphorisms appears to be an anonymous or a least pseudonymous work on the margins of Early Modern esotericism. As soon as we scratch the surface, however, some of the most important currents of the early seventeenth-century alchemical world begin to reveal themselves. We gain a glimpse into the royal courts, theological intrigues, universities, laboratories, publishing houses, and secret societies of central Europe. Curiously, the name that stands at the centre of these fascinating currents is perhaps only known to specialists of late-sixteenth and early-seventeenth century esotericism: Dr. RAPHÆL EGLINUS ICONIUS (1559–1622). Even among scholars he has remained quite obscure. 'For years he has stood on the periphery of discussions concerned with Renaissance occult traditions', remarks Bruce T. Moran in a pivotal study of mystical currents in the early seventeenth century; 'And yet in the light of what scarcely-known printed and archival sources actually reveal about him, Eglinus has to be considered one of the most important intellectual links supporting a Swiss-Italian and German connection within the mystical and alchemical history of the late sixteenth and early seventeenth centuries'.[1]

---

[1] Bruce T. MORAN, 'Alchemy, Prophecy, and the Rosicrucians: Raphæl Eglinus and Mystical Currents of the Early Seventeenth Century', in P. RATTANSI and A. CLERICUZIO, eds, *Alchemy and*

INTRODUCTION

As we will see, he not only rubbed shoulders with some of the most notable figures of this period, such as Giordano Bruno and Prince Moritz of Hessen, he was also directly connected to some of the most influential alchemical and early Rosicrucian publications. So who was Raphæl Eglinus?

Born in Götz (Münchhof, Switzerland), Eglinus was a Protestant theologian who rose to the Deaconship of the Cathedral of Zürich in the late sixteenth century.[2] Having arrived in Geneva in 1580 to study with the reformed theologian, Theodor Beza (1519–1605), he soon became enamoured with esoteric theories, and, much to Beza's frustration, temporarily absconded to Basel with a mysterious Italian teacher named Augustinus. Although it is uncertain whether this dalliance had anything to do with the heretical Italian philosopher, Giordano Bruno (1548–1600), who had recently visited Geneva, we know that Eglinus would later meet Bruno and attend the lectures that he gave in Zürich in 1591. Indeed, their connection was not merely peripheral; Bruno bequeathed the manuscript of these lectures— *De Entis Descensu* (On the Descent of Being)—to Eglinus to publish, and they subsequently appeared in 1595 as the *Summa Terminorum Metaphysicorum Jordani Bruni Nolani* (Summation of Metaphysical Terms by Giordano Bruno the Nolan).[3] It is therefore safe to assume that Eglinus's eso-

Chemistry in the 16th and 17th Centuries. Dordrecht, Springer, 1994, p. 103.

2   Our main source for the life of Eglinus is the excellent study by MORAN, 'Raphæl Eglinus and Mystical Currents of the Early Seventeenth Century', passim, which corrects the polemical account of John FERGUSON published in *Bibliotheca Chemica*, 1906; reprint, 1954, volume 1, pp. 232–33.

3   *Summa Terminorum metaphysicorum ad capessendum Logicæ et Philosophiæ studium, ex Iordani Bruni Nolani Entis descensu manusc. excerpta; nunc primum luci commissa; a Rephæle Eglino leonio, Tigurino.*

teric interests had taken firm root.

Rumoured to have turned to alchemy to pay for a complex accrual of debts, his involvement in the royal art embraced not only the operative but also the speculative dimensions of the Hermetic sciences. Indeed, according to his own account, alchemy was never in conflict with theology; rather, it was wholly consistent with a sophisticated inquiry into the depth of God's creation.⁴ But the popular perception of alchemy as fraudulent rather than philosophical persisted, perhaps exacerbated by the fact that he allegedly spent more time looking after his mining interests than his pastoral responsibilities. All of this served to complicate a separate, more serious set of suspicions that arose against him concerning apostasy. As a result of this, he was dismissed from his ecclesiastical position, and asked to leave Zürich.

Eglinus's apostasy and excommunication reveals the broader cultural fabric that must always be borne in mind when we attempt to grasp the wider religious context of early seventeenth century alchemy. In the German-speaking Europe of this period, alchemy was often embedded within a tacit polemic between Protestant and Catholic theological divides. That these were very real tensions is attested to by their dramatic eruption in the Thirty Years War (1616–1648), which would see deep religious rifts mercilessly exploited for raw political hegemony.⁵

    Tiguri, apud Ioannem Wolphium, 1595. See MORAN, 'Raphæl Eglinus', pp. 106–7.

4   MORAN, 'Raphæl Eglinus', pp. 105, 115 n. 9, citing: Letter to Obmann Hans Rudolf Rahn, 24 Nov. 1605; Staatsarchiv des Kantons Zürich: E I 1.6a.

5   For detailed context in relation to Eglinus, Elias Artista, Paracelsianism, and Rosicrucianism, see especially Captain NEMO and Fra' CERCONE's, *Philalethe Reveal'd*, vol. 2, Nautilus Editions & Alla Via Jacobea Editions, 2016, pp. 120–207.

Fortunately for Eglinus, his excommunication was mitigated by the assistance of the Zürich city council, who put him in touch with the court of the German Prince, Moritz of Hessen (1572–1632), who, in 1606, appointed Eglinus to the faculty of theology at the University of Marburg. Perhaps second only to Rudolf II of Prague, Prince Moritz of Hessen was one of the most important patrons of the Hermetic sciences in Renaissance Europe. Gathering a sizeable circle of alchemical confidants about him, his court drew notable visits from Rudold II's circle at Prague, including luminaries such as Dr. John Dee and Count Michæl Maier. Prince Moritz corresponded widely with many alchemical authorities, collected a library of alchemical manuscripts, and fostered laboratory research into iatrochemistry and chrysopoeia. More than this, however, the Prince participated in an alchemical vision of a renovated society beyond the sectarian divisions of his time, a vision that would come to inform the Rosicrucian manifestos of 1614–1615.[6]

Eglinus was thus well placed, and it was precisely here that the *Basilian Aphorisms* would be published. But before we turn to the edition history of this curious text, it is first necessary to trace some of Eglinus's alchemical interests in more detail.

From around 1600, Eglinus corresponded with the Swiss physician and philologist, Jacob Zwinger (1569–1610). The letters that he exchanged with Zwinger, who had a deep interest in iatrochemistry, give us a detailed insight into Eglinus's alchemical preoccupations.[7] Among other things, they reveal how Eglinus's theories were especially influenced by Alexander von Suchten's 1570 work, *De secretis antimonii*

---

6   See H. WATANABE-O'KELLY's remarks in *Court Culture in Dresden*, London, Palgrave Macmillan, 2002, p. 106.
7   Per MORAN's summary in 'Raphæl Eglinus', pp. 105–106.

(On the Mystery of Antimony).[8] The emphasis on antimony naturally alerts us to themes that would appear in a work published some years later under the name of Basilius Valentinus: *Triumph Wagen Antimonii* (*The Triumphal Chariot of Antimony*, 1604). Consolidating the Valentinian motif, Eglinus also mentions two manuscripts allegedly written in Basilius's own hand, in which two techniques—one for extracting the sulphur of gold; one for making potable gold—are described.[9] In discussing these procedures, he draws heavily on Paracelsus.[10]

But it is in Marburg that the Basilian motif would begin to surface more explicitly. In 1612, Eglinus would publish a small volume called the *Cheiragogia Heliana de Auro philosophico necdum cognito* (A Manuduction to the Philosopher's Magical Gold),[11] in which he summarises Valentinus's work, discusses the preparation of his 'stone of fire' from mercury of antimony and the vitriol of copper and iron, as well as a procedure for opening metals using a preparation

---

8 Strassburg, Ch. Müllers Erben, 1570.
9 In addition to von Suchten, Eglinus was influenced by the works of Johannes Baptista Montanus (1498–1551), Marcellus Palingenius (fl. 1528), and Petrus Bonus (fourteenth century); he also alludes to private contact with figures such as Scotus Comes (Alexander Sidonius/Seton) and Angelo Sala. See MORAN, 'Raphæl Eglinus', pp. 105–6.
10 MORAN, 'Raphæl Eglinus', pp. 106.
11 Marburg: Rudolph Hutwelcher, 1612. The full title of the English translation, published in 1659, and attributed to 'Geo. Thor. Astromagus', reads: *Cheiragogia heliana: A manuduction to the philosopher's magical gold: out of which profound, and subtile discourse; two of the particullar tinctures, that of Saturn and Jupiter conflate; and of Jupiter single, are recommended as short and profitable works, by the restorer of it to the light. To which is added; Antron Mitras; Zoroaster's cave: or, An intellectuall echo, &c. Together with the famous Catholic epistle of John Pontanus upon the minerall fire.*

made from common salt.¹² But in the meantime the *Aphorisms* would appear, first in a work without any explicit connection to Valentinus; second, in an edition that would be explicitly linked to him.

BASILIUS VALENTINUS

The figure of Basilius Valentinus is presented as a fifteenth century Benedictine monk from Erfurt, Germany. Under this name, a series of influential alchemical works appeared between 1599 and 1604. These include *Ein kurtz summarischer Tractat, von dem grossen Stein der Uralten* (A Short Summary Tract of the Great Stone of the Ancients, 1599/1602), featuring the famous *Zwölf Schlüssel* (Twelve Keys), and *Triumph Wagen Antimonii* (Triumphal Chariot of Antimony, 1604).

Since the early eighteenth century, however, the validity of the Valentinian persona has come into question. In 1729, J. Ch. Motschmann wrote:

> *Ich habe anfangs bey mir angestanden, dieses Mannes in meinen gelehrten Erfurth Erwehnung zu thun, weilen verschiedene Autores glauben, er sei niemals in Erfurth, oder wohl gar in der Welt gewesen*
>
> In the beginning I had hesitated to make mention of this man in my study of Erfurt's literature, because numerous authors believe that he was never in Erfurt at all, nor even the world.¹³

---

12 MORAN, 'Raphæl Eglinus', p. 106.
13 J. Ch. MOTSCHMANN, *Erfordia Literata*, Erfurt, 1729, p. 396.

Frater Basilius Valentinus
Chymische Schriften, 1717

By the late nineteenth century, mounting evidence against a fifteenth-century compostion of the Valentinian corpus was presented by historians of chemistry such as Hermann Kopp. Following suit, scholars of alchemy now typically regard the corpus as composed, wholly or partly, by the editor Johann Thölde (c. 1565–1614), a salinist from Frankenhausen. Indeed, Thölde's own work, the *Haligraphia* (Writings on Salt, 1603)[14] bears a particularly close resemblance to Valentine's *Letzes Testament* (Last Testament, 1626).[15]

Although it seems evident that Thölde composed the works himself, perhaps with some collaborators, it is also possible that some fragments of genuine material, elaborated upon by Thölde and his collaborators, formed the basis of the works. The existence of genuine fragments is suggested by Eglinus and others, who claim to have possessed manuscripts written in Valentinus' own hand.[16] Whatever the case, it is likely that Thölde did not work alone, and given that the major works attributed to Valentinus appeared precisely in the period that Eglinus was active (i.e. just before he published the *Aphorisms* at Marburg), the possibility exists that Eglinus may have been involved in the compositions himself. To what extent this can be verified remains

14 Johann THÖLDE, *Haligraphia, Das ist, Gründliche und eigendliche Beschreibung aller Saltz Mineralien : Darin von deß Saltzes erster Materia, Ursprung, Geschlecht, Unterscheid, Eigenschafft ... gehandelt wird ; Beneben einer Historischen Beschreibung aller Saltzwercke ... ; Auch wie man aus allen Metallen und vornembsten Mineralien ... ihre Saltz außziehen, und zu Menschlicher Gesundheit brauchen sol*, Leipzig, Apel, 1603.

15 Hermann KOPP, *Beiträge zur Geschichte der Chemie*, Braunschweig, 1869–1875; Allen G. DEBUS, 'Basil Valentine', in *Dictionary of Scientific Biography*, vol. 13, New York, Scribner's, 1976; *The Chemical Philosophy*, pp. 94 ff.

16 MORAN, 'Raphæl Eglinus', p. 106.

to be seen; but if Eglinus's views influenced the Valentinian compositions, we can certainly look to the emphasis on antimony as a source of the metallic essence (per von Suchten), and its influence on Eglinus, as a fruitful line of inquiry. What we do know for certain is that he was involved in the translation and transmisson of alchemical works which purport to be written by Valentinus.

HISTORY & PROVENANCE OF THE APHORISMS
First Edition: Helia Artiſta (1608)

Composed in Latin under the ægis of a certain 'Heliophilo Philochemico', the first edition of our Hermetic Canons was published at Marburg in 1608. It appeared towards the end of a larger work entitled *Disquisitio de Helia Artista*, the full title of which reads:

> *Disquisitio de Helia Artista, in qua de metallorum transformatione adversus Hagelii et Pererii Jesuitarum opiniones, evidenter et solide disseritur. Editio postrema correctior et melior. Accesserunt recens Canones Hermetici de Spiritu, Anima et Corpore majoris et minoris Mundi, cum appendice. Marpurgi, Typis Hutwelckerianis, 1608.*

> Disquisition by Helia Artista, in which the transformation of metals is clearly and firmly asserted against the opinions of the Jesuits Hagelus and Pereius. Corrected and improved from the previous edition. Comes with the recent Hermetic Canons of the Spirit, Soul, and Body of the Major and Minor World, and appendices. Marburg, Printed by Hutwelcker, 1608.

In this edition, it should be noted that our Hermetic Aphorisms are not yet designated as 'Basilian'. This would occur the following year, in the 1609 edition. But before we turn to that, it is first necessary to unpack the context provided by this 1608 edition. The 'Helia Artista' referred to in the title of the *Disquisitio* refers to a figure anticipated as a kind of 'prophet' of the alchemical arts. Alluding to the Biblical Elias (Elijah), who was raised to heaven in a fiery whirlwind before being destined to return as the herald of the Messiah, the roots of the Helia Artista motif probably tap into Jewish traditions from fifteenth-century Spain, where the Messiah was conceived as a kind of alchemist.[17] Its most pronounced branches, however, stem from statements made by Paracelsus, who considered himself a *novus Elias*, or at the very least, presented himself as a sort of a 'Jean the Baptist' of a coming alchemical messiah.[18] 'Much art is still withheld from us', he writes in his *Von den natürlichen Dingen* (On Natural Things, 1525), for 'to transform iron into copper is less than turning iron into gold, and despite the little that God has revealed, more still is hidden, until the time of the Art of Helias, who is to come'.[19]

Early Paracelsians would perpetuate the theme. Gerhard Dorn (c. 1530–1584), one of the earliest editors and commentators of Paracelsus, and an important alchemical theorist in his own right, saw in the coming of Elias Artista 'the moment when nothing that is hidden will fail to be revealed'.[20] In a similar vein, the Prussian alchemist, Alex-

---

17 Anoine FAIVRE, 'Elie Artiste, our le messie des philosophes de la nature (première partie)', *Aries* 3.1, p. 120.
18 FAIVRE, 'Elie Artiste', pp. 121–22.
19 PARACELSUS, *De Mineralibus*, ch. 8, in Abt. 1, 16; cited in FAIVRE, 'Elie Artiste', p. 122.
20 DORN, *De transmutatione metallorum*, in *Theatrum Chemicum*, vol. 1, Strasbourg, 1602, pp. 610, 662; cited in FAIVRE, 'Elie Artiste', p. 123.

ander von Suchten (1520–1575), whose works, as we have seen, influenced Eglinus, would write that the meaning of all the known books of magic would remain hidden until the coming of Helias.[21]

Whatever the exact provenance of the Elias Artista theme, the text in which our *Aphorisms* first appeared has the distinction of being the first book to explicitly place the figure of Elias Artista in its title. With the turn of the seventeenth century, in the wake of the religious renovation signaled by the Reformation, a new esoteric current would emerge—Rosicrucianism—a development to which our text's author would also prove closely bound. Indeed, the Elias motif would prove to be one of the major threads feeding and informing the coming ferment of Rosicrucianism, some of whose formative texts Eglinus himself has been closely connected to. 'It may have been Eglinus', remarks Moran, 'who, just a year earlier, wrote another work on hieroglyphics and magical signs under the pseudonyms Philip a Gabala and Philemon R.C.':

> This work, called the *Consideratio Brevis*, appeared with the first publication of the Rosicrucian manifesto, the *Confessio Fraternitatis*, at Kassel in 1615. By then, the best known Rosicrucian text, the *Fama Fraternitatis* (1614), had also appeared, published, as was the *Confessio*, by the Kassel publisher Wilhelm Wessel. Deep in Eglinus's correspondence with Moritz lies an undated reference to a "little treatise" that Eglinus had written and which might possibly have come to Wessel, who had just published the *Fama*.[22]

---

21 Alexander von Suchten, *De secretis antimonii*, Basel, 1570, ch. 3, p. 22; cited in Faivre, 'Elie Artiste', p. 123.
22 Moran, 'Raphæl Eglinus', p. 112.

While Moran rightly acknowledges that the *Fama* and *Confessio* appear to be connected more with the Tübingen circle, he makes a plausible case for the emergence of the *Consideratio Brevis* from the court of Prince Moritz, and thus the likely role of Eglinus.[23]

A Defense of Alchemy

As its title indicates, in addition to the prophetic theme, the book also provides a defense of the art of alchemy against the opinions of the Jesuit Balthasar Hagelius, a professor of philosophy at the University of Ingolstadt who published a work entitled *De Metallo et Lapide* (On Metals and Stones, 1588). Hagel criticised the traditional sulphur-mercury theory of metallogenesis by calling attention to the lack of these substances in the earth's metallic veins. The *Disquisitio* responded by maintaining the positions of metallurgical and chemical authorities such as Georgius Agricola (1494–1555), Andreas Libavius (1555–1616), and Christoph Entzelt (1517–1583): i.e., that by the time metals had formed in the veins of the earth, the formative sulphur and mercury had already been fully integrated into the metallic body. Eglinus also countered Hagelius' critique of the metallic transmutation theory. Against the position that all metals are essentially different, and could not therefore be transmuted into one another, Eglinus maintained the alchemical view that metals were variations of one species. Their apparent differences were only due to the purity and proportion of their constituent sulphur and mercury.[24] Because the metals were of one essential nature, they could be transformed into each

---

23   MORAN, 'Raphæl Eglinus', pp. 112 ff.
24   MORAN, 'Raphæl Eglinus', pp. 107–108.

other by modulating the purity and proportion of their principles.

Second Edition: Basilius Valentinus (1609)

In 1609, one year after the first edition, another work appeared containing our Hermetic Aphorisms, this time qualified as 'Basilian':

> *De Microcosmo: Deque magno mundi mysterio et medicina hominis liber geminus, Magni Basilii Valentini, quondam ordinis benedictini philosophi germani: Exterorum in gratiam recens, ab Angelo Medico latinitate donatus, cum interpretis aphorismis Basilianis et præfatione philosophica, to Illustriss. Celsissimumque Principem Dn. Augustum Anhaltinum &c. Marpurgi, Typis Guolgangi Kezelii, 1609*

A book on the mystery of the microcosm, the great mystery of the world, and the healing of man, by the Great Basil Valentine, philosopher of the German Benedictine Order, freshly and freely rendered into Latin from the foreign [tongue] by Angelus Medicus, with the Basilian Aphorisms, by the translator, and a philosophical preface dedicated to our highest and most illustrious lord, Prince Augustus von Anhalt. Published in Marburg by Wolfgang Kezelius, 1609.[25]

25 The text of the *Aphorisms* appears here as a supplement to a Latin translation by Eglinus of an originally *German* work by Valentinus, entitled: *De Microcosmo, oder von den kleinen Welt des menschlichen Leibes, Fr. Basili Valentini, Benedictiner Ordens, was solche in sich hält, woraus sie zusammen gebaut, und was ihr ganzer Begriff und Inhalt vermag, sammt ihrem Ende und Ausgang, allen so den Grund der Weisheit lieben, das Vornehmst, und zu wissen höchlich vonnöthen.* (On the Microcosm, or on the small world of the human body,

This extended title tells us that the Latin text of the Aphorisms was composed by a certain 'Angelus Medicus'. According to Massimo Marra, who has written an important introduction to a recent Italian translation of the Aphorisms, Angelus Medicus was one of many pseudonyms used by Eglinus. Although the expression *angelus medicus* ('healing angel', or 'angel of medicine') was a known Latin epithet of the Archangel Raphæl, here it clearly alludes to Eglinus's Christian name, Raphæl.[26] Indeed, as a theologian and Paracelsian, Eglinus would have been most partial to the connections his own name bore to iatrochemistry—the alchemical art of healing through the use of mineral, metallic, and botanic arcana.

In this 1609 edition, the name 'Hermophilo Philochemico' (Friend of Hermes, Friend of Chymistry/Alchemy) is given as the original compiler of the *Aphorisms*, evoking in form the Heliophilo (Friend of Helios/Friend of the Sun) of the 1608 edition. Both of these names turn out to be *noms de plume* for Eglinus. As will be seen in the commentary, the text of the Aphorisms itself also has further allusions to the name Raphæl Eglinus Iconius in the initials R. E. I., which provide an epigraph to the volume.

---

by Frater Basilius Valentinus, of the Benedictine Order; What it contains, what it is made out of, and what its entire concept and content is capable of, together with its demise and departure, all to love the ground of wisdom, and to be called to know the highest).

26   Massimo MARRA, ed., and Michela BRINDISI, trans., 'Gli aforismi basiliani di Eglinus Iconius (Angelus Medicus). Simbolismo ermetico e influenze paracelsiane in un testo alchemico seicentesco', *Abstracta*.

The Theatrum Chemicum; European Translations

In 1613, three of Eglinus's treatises were published by Lazarus Zetzner in volume four of his monumental *Theatrum Chemicum*.[27] Despite the fact that Eglinus used several pseudonyms and anagrams when publishing his work, the *Cheiragogia* (by 'Nicolai Niger Hopelius'), the *Disquisitio* (by Raphæl Eglinus Iconius), and the *Aphorismi Basiliani* (by 'Hermophilus Philochemicus') appeared together in succession, tacitly confirming their common authorship.

In 1661, a French translation of the Aphorisms by an alchemist named Father Gabriel de Castaigne (c. 1562–c. 1630) appeared as *Aphorismes Basiliens, ou Canons Hermétiques de l'esprit et de l'ame, comme aussi du corps mitoyen du grand et petit monde*. In 1901, this translation reappeared in an edition by the erudite *fin-de-siècle* esotericist, Emile Grillot de Givry (1874–1929). De Givry's edition was a more or less verbatim reprinting of the 1661 version, and Givry was apparently well aware that de Castaigne was not the original author of the text. The publishers of this re-edition were the infamous Brothers Chacornac, who operated the chief esoteric publishing house in France during the Parisian alchemical revival. From this matrix, modern luminaries such as Fulcanelli, Pierre Dujols, and René Schwaller de Lubicz would emerge. In more recent years, an Italian translation by Michela Brindisi appeared together with an introduction and notes by Massimo Marra, entitled *Gli aforismi basiliani di Eglinus Iconius (Angelus Medicus). Simbolismo ermetico e influenze paracelsiane in un testo alchemico seicentesco*.

---

27 *Theatrum Chemicum*, Argentorati, Lazari Zetzneri Bibliopolae, 1613, volume 4: *Cheiragogia Heliana*, pp. 299–323; *Disquisitio Heliana, de metallorum transformatione*, pp. 326–67; *Aphorismi Basiliani*, pp. 368–71.

The present English edition, edited and translated by Doctors Mirco A. Manucci and Aaron Cheak, is based on the Latin text of the 1608/1609 edition. In making our translation, we have naturally consulted the French and Italian editions, and have had the benefit of having our translation thoroughly checked by the best Latinists we know: Professor Riccardo Di Giuseppe, and Michael A. Putman. Any lingering errors or misinterpretations are, of course, the responsibility of the editors alone.

AARON CHEAK

TEXT

TRANSLATION

APHORISMI BASILIANI
SIVE
CANONES HERMETICI
DE
SPIRITU, ANIMA, ET CORPORE
MAJORIS & MINORIS MUNDI,

Conscripti ab

HERMOPHILO
PHILOCHEMICO

Ter Maximus Hermes

Ταῦτά μὲν ἐννοῦντι ἀληθῆ δόξειεν ἄν,
αγνοοῦνζε δὲ ἄπιστα.

*Hæc scienti quidem vera videantur;
Ignoranti verò incredibilia.*

MARPVRGI
Ex Officina Guolgangi Kezelii

M.DC.VIII.

THE BASILIAN APHORISMS
OR
HERMETIC CANONS

OF THE
SPIRIT, SOUL, AND BODY
OF THE MAJOR & MINOR WORLD

Collected by

HERMOPHILO
PHILOCHEMICO

Thrice Great Hermes

Ταυτά μὲν ἐννοῦντι ἀληθῆ δόξειεν ἄν,
αγνοοῦνζε δὲ ἄπιστα.

*Let these things to the knower appear true;
to the ignorant incredible*

MARBURG
From the Atelier of Wolfgang Kezelius

1608

Canones Hermetici
de Spiritu, Anima, et Corpore
Majoris & Minoris Mundi

I.

HERMES τρισμέγιστος *ob triplicis regni Mineralis, Vegetabilis, Animalis, imo ob triplicis in una creata essentia subsistentiæ indagationem, in qua vim omnem vegetabilis, animalis et mineralis Naturæ exploravit, Pater Philosophorum dici meruit.*

The Hermetic Canons
Of the Spirit, Soul, and Body
Of the Major & Minor World

I.

HERMES *trismegistos* deserved to be called Father of the Philosophers for investigating the triple kingdom, Mineral, Vegetable, and Animal, indeed for studying the triple subsistence in one created essence, in which he explored all virtues of the vegetable, animal, and mineral Nature.

2.

Vis vegetans in natura Mercurii volantis, instar nivis candidi, concreti, non vulgaris inest; qui tam majoris, quam minoris mundi quidam Spiritus est, unde naturæ ipsius humanæ, secundum animam rationalem, pendet mobilitas, atque fluxibilitas.

2.

The vegetating force in the nature of the volatile Mercury lies in the likeness of a candid, concrete, uncommon snow, which is a certain Spirit of the major as well as the minor world, whence depends the mobility and fluidity of the same human nature, according to the rational soul.

3.

Animans autem vis, tanquam Mundi glutinum, inter Spiritum atque corpus medium est, atque utriusque vinculum, in Sulphure nimirum rubentis atque transparentis olei cujusdam, veluti Soli in Majore Mundo et cor Microcosmi.

3.

On the other hand, the animating force, as a glue of the World, is a medium between Spirit and body, and their reciprocal bond, without a doubt in the Sulphur of a certain reddish and transparent oil, like the Sun in the Major World and the heart of the Microcosm.

4.

*Mineralitas denique tanquam corpus in-
star Salis obtinet, mirabilis virtutis et odo-
ris, ubi sal a scoria terræ separatum fuerit,
a Mercurio non nisi corporis crassitie, et
consistentia terræ distans.*

4.

Finally, minerality obtains a body in the guise of a Salt of remarkable virtue and smell, where salt from the earthly scoria shall be separated, not dissimilar to Mercury, except for the coarseness of the body and the consistency of the earth.

5.

Hæ tres subsistentiæ in una creata essentia limbum minoris et majoris mundi constituunt, ex quo formatus est primus homo, cum fingeretur e pulvere terræ. Huc accedit anima rationalis Microcosmi immortalis a Deo immediate inspirata, horum trium et omnium functionum in homine motrix atque directrix causa, veluti Regina.

5.

These three subsistences in one created essence constitute the limbus of the minor and major world, from which the first man was formed, having been shaped from the dust of the earth. Here enters the rational soul of the immortal Microcosm, immediately inspired by God, the moving and directing cause, like a Queen, of those three and all other functions.

6.

Cæterum ut è quatuor elementis conglobato pulvere terræ vis corporum nostrorum atque vita integra est, si spiritus Mercurialis, tanquam humidum radicale, & anima sulphurea, tanquam calidum naturale, una cum salis consistentia à putredine asservantis, suaviter in unum conspirent: ita vice versa animam immortalem à corpore conglobati pulveris terræ separari necesse est, si vel in uno principiorum trium pluribusve defectus oboriatur: in toto quidem unde mors; in parte vero, unde morbus: quod in septem Principalium membrorum anatomia præcipue videre est.

6.

Moreover just as the vigour and life of our bodies is kept whole and sound due to the dust of the earth which has been coagulated from the four elements, and if the spirit of Mercury (the radical humidity), the sulphuric soul (the natural heat), together with the consistency of salt (which preserves from putrefaction) sweetly harmonise in one thing, then so *vice versa*: it is necessary to separate the immortal soul from the body of the conglobated dust of the earth, if in one or more of the three principles a defect is found. If this deficiency is in all principles, then death comes; if only in some, sickness ensues; which is mostly seen in the anatomy of the principal seven organs.

7.

Huic triplici defectui nihil æque mederi potest, quam illa limbi, ex quo primus homo conflatus est, conglobata in unum e ternis principiis massa, quæ ad quamvis naturæ potentiam atque vim excitandam ac fovendam valet, si in corpus astrale fixum debite fuerit versa.

7.

Nothing can remedy this triple defect as adequately as that mass of the limbus, conglobated from three principles into one, from which the first man was animated, which is exceedingly capable of rousing and nourishing the power and virtue of nature, if it will be duly turned in a fixed astral body

8.

Ex quo intelligitur Balſamum ſubjecti Hermetici cum corpore humano ſingularem harmoniam habere: unde Helveticus ille Physicorum Monarcha PHILIPPUS AB HOHENHEIM *ſive* PARACELSUS, *libro de Lapide Physico, Manuali dicto, hac Medicina Microcosmum, qui in limbo terræ ſitus et ex pulvere terræ formatus eſt,* RADICALITER TANQUAM A SUO SIMILI, *non autem ſecundum opinionem, ſed vere ac proprie ad ſanitatem poſſe perduci et conſervari, rectiſſime asserit.*

8.

From that can be understood that the Balsam of the Hermetic subject has a singular harmony with the human body: thence, that Swiss Monarch of the Physicians, PHILIP VON HOHENHEIM alias PARACELSUS, in the book on the Physical Stone, named *The Manual*, rightly affirms that this Medicine, not by opinion, but truly and properly can, RADICALLY AS SOMETHING OF THE SAME KIND, lead, preserve, and restore health to the Microcosm, which is located in the limbus of the Earth and was formed from the dust of earth.

9.

Tanto vero id magis attendum est, quanto medicina vulgaris debilior est ad tria illa principia microcosmi, eorundemque harmoniam radicaliter tuendam atque instruendam: quippe veluti ex accidenti (quandoquidem tota fere in quatuor humoribus occupatur) tribus illis principiis obstetricans.

9.

Truly, the greater the attention we pay to it, the weaker this common medicine is in radically keeping and directing the three principles of the microcosm and their reciprocal harmony: in fact (because it is almost wholly occupied with the four humours) it only helps give birth from the three principles indirectly.

10.

Mineralis autem Medicina Chymica e metallis et mineralibus raro vel recte paratur vel administratur: unde Paracelsus eodem in libro Medicinam suam omnibus præfert: negare tamen sese negat, magna Arcana item aliis in rebus Mineralibus inesse, sed longioris operæ et laboris, neque facile recte usurpari, præsertim ab imperitioribus; qui in hæc incidentes plus damni dent, quam prodesse queant.

10.

Instead, the Mineral Chemical Medicine is rarely prepared and administered in the proper way from metals and minerals: hence Paracelsus in his book prefers his Medicine to all others. Nevertheless, he does not deny that great Arcana are inside other mineral things, but they require longer and more laborious work, and are not easily conquerable in a correct way, especially by amateurs; for when they come upon such matters, they often end up doing more harm than good.

II.

Quæramus igitur Limbum Microcosmi in quo is situs est; hoc est, globum illum viscidum terræ, ex Mercurio, Sulphure, et Sale concretum: qui quidem quoniam ex humido quodam existit, pulchre viscosa humiditatis humiditas, secundum Gebrum, dici potest.

II.

Let us then search the Limbus of the Microcosm, in which it is situated; that is, that viscid globe of earth, made concrete from Mercury, Sulphur, and Salt: which because it comes into being from a certain humidity, can eloquently be called the viscid humidity of humidity, according to Geber.

12.

Sicuti enim Mundus licet ex Nihilo conditus, originem debet Aquæ, cui Spiritus Domini incubabat: rebus tam Cœlestibus quam Terrestribus omnibus inde prodeuntibus: ita Limbus hic emergit ex Aqua non vulgari, neque ex rore cœlesti, aut ex Aëre condensato in cavernis Terræ, vel in Recipiente ipso, non ex abysso Maris, fontibus, puteis, fluminibusve hausto: sed ex Aqua quadam perpessa, omnibus obvia; paucissimis cognita; Que in se habet, quæcunque ad totius operis complementum sunt ei necessaria, omni a moto extrinseco.

12.

In fact, as the world has originated from Nothing, it owes its origin to Water, upon which the Spirit of the Lord lay: thence come forth all things, celestial and terrestrial alike. So, here emerges the Limbus from an uncommon Water, neither drawn from the celestial dew, nor from Air condensed in the caverns of the Earth, nor in the recipient itself, neither from the abyss of the Sea, nor from fountains, wells, or rivers, but from a certain Water over which we have laboured, which is ready at hand to everybody, but understood by very few. It possesses everything it needs for the completion of the entire work within itself, save for any external motion.

13.

Est autem Natura hæc quædam media inter Majorem et Minorem Mundum ubique repertita, et tam ad pauperem, quam ad divitem: uti adferunt omnes Philosophi. Projicitur enim in viis, et conculcatur pedibus: licet tam admirandarum operationum sit fons. Unde tria illa corporis nostri principia, diversis proprietatibus gaudentia, sunt instauranda.

13.

Nevertheless, Nature is a certain medium between the Higher and Lower World, to be found everywhere, by both poor and rich alike, as all Philosophers attest. It is thrown into the streets, and trampled under feet, yet it is the fountain of admirable operations. Thence the three principia of our body, enjoying diverse properties, are to be restored.

14.

Hæc materia resoluta in suam propriam Aquam (ab Aqua enim omnis Generatio profluit.) per 4. Elementa rotatur, donec in Naturam Astralem fixam abeat, in Ovo Physico; quod a fotu Gallinæ indesinenter ovis incubantis dicitur: alioqui spes omnis sobolis periret.

14.

This matter, dissolved into its proper Water (for all generation comes forth from Water) is rotated across the four Elements, till it will be turned into a fixed Astral Matter, in a physical Egg, which is called so after the warmth of a Hen constantly incubating the egg: else, all hope of birth would die.

15.

Sic Avis Hermetis semel inclusa Caveæ, quæ Furnus est, vaporosi ignis nostri calore continuato gradatim excitanda est, donec seipsam excludat, et suo partu omnes sanet.

15.

Thus the Hermetic Bird once locked inside the Cave, which is the Oven, is to be roused gradually by the continuous heat of our vaporous fire, till it opens up and heals everything with its birth.

16.

Ut autem in trium Principiorum perpessæ hujus Aquæ præparatione nihil addimus substantiali Materiei, nihilque subsistentibus tribus proprietatibus in ea adimimus, sed sola præparatione superflua removemus, hoc est, heterogenea, sive Terram emortuam, et aquam insipidam: ita opus Hermeticum trium Principiorum præparatorum conjunctione inchoatur sub certa proportione, nempe pondere corporis sesquialtera parte Spiritum Animamque propemodum æquantis.

16.

However, in the preparation of the three Principia of this troubled Water, we do not add to the substantial Matter, nor do we subtract anything from the three properties subsistent in it; we remove only the superfluous, namely the heterogeneous, like the dried Earth and the insipid water; so the Hermetic work is begun by the conjunction of the three Principles under a certain proportion, indeed with the weight of the body almost equal to the sesquialter part of spirit and soul

17.

Exinde fotu continuo regenda sunt omnia, ut Natura Agens interior, neque cessent, neque excessum patiatur. Fiat igitur initio ignis mitis, et primus quidem quasi 4. guttarum sive filorum: donec Materia nigrescat. Post adde, ut sit quasi 14. filorum: donec se abluat, et Iris apparens in colorem Gryseum desinat. Inde urge quasi 24. filis, usque ad Albedinem perfectam, Nive superiorem, fluentem, fixam, quæ est Luna Microcosmi.

17.

Afterwards all things have to be regulated by a continuous heat, so that the Agent inside Nature neither stops, nor suffers an excess. Let there be a mild fire in the beginning, initially of 4 drops or threads, till the Matter becomes black. Then add almost 14 threads, till it washes itself, and the appearing Iris ends in a Grey colour. Then persevere with almost 24 threads, till a perfect Albedo [appears], superior to Snow, fluid and fixed, which is the Moon of the Microcosm.

18.

Quod si procedere cupis ad Rubedinem perfectam, per dies 70. continuabis ignem, donec Lapis vertatur in Rubinum pellucidum gravem, atque ponderosum: qui quidem est Sol Microcosmi, eodem modo augmentandus, quo fuit inchoatus. Hujus unum granum, sex mille granis æquipollet: unde in tenuissima Dosi est administrandus.

18.

Thus, if you wish to proceed to the perfect Rubedo, you will maintain your fire for 70 days, till the Stone is turned into a translucent Ruby of great weight, which is indeed the Sun of the Microcosm, to be augmented in the same way as when it was begun. A grain of this is equivalent to six-thousand grains, therefore is to be administered in a very small dose.

RADIX ELIXIRIS

Δ.
R.   E.
I.

Entheus est olli vigor et cœlestis imago,
Unde fluit nobis hæc
medicina Dei.

FINIS

ROOT OF THE ELIXIR

<pre>
         Δ.
   R.   E.
         I.
</pre>

The vigor and the celestial image
is inspired of that one, whence flows this
medicine of God.

END

Annotations and Commentary

Title page

The Basilian Aphorisms, or Hermetic Canons of the Spirit, Soul, and Body of the Major & Minor World, Collected by Hermophilo Philochemico. Thrice Great Hermes: 'Let these things to the knower appear true; to the ignorant incredible'. Marburg. From the Atelier of Wolfgang Kezelius, 1608.

The Balisian Aphorisms (*Aphorismi Basiliani*) were composed in Latin under the ægis of 'Hermophilo Philochemico', a pseudonym meaning 'Friend of Hermes, Friend of Chymistry/Alchemy)'. The aphorisms first appeared in 1608 as a supplement to a work published by Raphæl Eglinus Iconius; the following year it was republished in a Latin edition of BASILIUS VALENTINUS's *De Microcosmo* (On the Microcosm), which was also published by Eglinus.[1] It is here that the aphorisms first appeared with the designation 'Basilian'.

The title itself—the *Basilian* aphorisms—is thus a clear reference to Basil Valentine, a legendary monk from the Benedictine Priory of Saint Peter in Erfurt who was said to have composed his texts in the fifteenth century. Most researchers now agree that the works of Basilius were com-

---

[1] Marburg, Wolfgang Kezelius, 1609.

posed by Johann Thölde (1565–1614/1624), a German salt manufacturer who published the oldest text attributed to Valentinus in 1599: *Ein kurtz summarischer Tractat, von dem grossen Stein der Uralten* (A Short Summary Treatise on the Great Stone of the Ancients).[2] A number of influential alchemical works were published under Basilius's name, including the famous *Zwölf Schlüssel* (Twelve Keys) and *Triumph Wagen Antimonii* (Triumphal Chariot of Antimony); the lion's share of his writings were compiled in a 1677 text entitled *Chymische Schriften* (Alchemical Writings).

It is worth adding that the name Basilius itself derives from the Greek word for 'king', βασιλεύς (*basileus*). The 'Basilian Aphorisms' are therefore not merely Valentinian, they are 'kingly' or 'royal' aphorisms. This meaning not only underscores the image of alchemy as a royal art (*ars regia*), but also emphasises the leitmotif of the book itself, in which three *kingdoms* constitute the triadic structure of reality in accordance with Hermetic and Paracelsian thought.

Indeed, the subtitle: *The Hermetic Canons of the Spirit, Soul, and Body of the Major & Minor World*, alludes to the divine, threefold structure of reality that operates both in the world at large (*mundus major*, or macrocosm), and in the human psychosomatic complex (*mundus minor*, or microcosm). The predominance of this theme is evident from its assertion in the title as well as in the very first canon, which purports to explain the meaning of Hermes as 'Thrice-Great' (*trismegistos*) by reference to the three kingdoms of nature as well as the 'triple subsistence in once created essence' (*triplicis in una creata essentia subsistentiæ*).

The homology of macrocosm and microcosm expressed here may be traced with fair precision to the Hermetic phi-

---

2   On Thölde, see Gerhard GÖRMAR, 'Johann Thölde, Herausgeber der Schriften des „Basilius Valentinus" und Verfasser der *Haliographia*—eine biographische Skizze', *Mitteilung* 16, 2002, 3–19.

ANNOTATIONS AND COMMENTARY 75

losophy of Late Antiquity, which explicitly states: 'God [...] has two forms, cosmos and anthropos'.³ More generally, the motif can be discerned in the cosmology of Plato's *Timæus*, in which the human *pneuma*, *psychē*, and *sōma* (πνευμα, ψυχη, σωμα) mirror the spirit, soul, and body of the cosmos. As scholars such as Algis Uždavinys and Erik Iversen have shown, the deeper roots of this Platonic and Hermetic motif are discernable in Egyptian theology and cosmology, (even though it would be a stretch to suggest that this was concretely known by figures such as Eglinus).⁴

Consolidating the ancient Hermetic motif, the Greek text on the title page, attributed to the 'Thrice Great Hermes' (i.e., Hermes Trismegistus), appears to be adapted from a discourse of the *Corpus Hermeticum* entitled 'Hermes Trismegistus, Concerning Thought and Sense'. The specific passage reads:

> Ταῦτά σοι, Ἀσκληπιέ, ἐννοῦντι ἀληθῆ δόξειεν ἄν, νοοῦντι δὲ ἄπιστα · τῷ γὰρ νοῆσαι ἕπεται τὸ πιστεῦσαι, τὸ ἀπιστῆσαι δὲ τῷ μὴ νοῆσαι.
>
> O Asclepius, these things will seem true to you if you understand them, but if you remain ignorant they are beyond belief. To understand them is to take them as true, and not to understand is to take them as untrue.⁵

---

3   *Corpus Hermeticum*, Asclepius 1.10 (SCOTT, 304-5): 'Aeternitatis dominus deus primus est, secundus est mundus, homo est tertius [...] cuis sunt imagines duae mundus et homo'.
4   Algis UŽDAVINYS, *Philosophy as a Rite of Rebirth: From Ancient Egypt to Neoplatonism*, Wiltshire, Prometheus Trust, 2008; Erik IVERSEN, *Egyptian and Hermetic Doctrine*, Copenhagen, Museum Tusculanum Press, 1984.
5   *Corpus Hermeticum* IX, § 10, trans. Salaman.

The Latin quotation that follows is a pithy translation of the Greek:

Hæc scienti quidem vera videantur;
Ignoranti verò incredibilia.

Let these things to the knower appear true;
to the ignorant incredible.

Canon I

Hermes Trismegistos deserved to be called Father of the Philosophers for investigating the triple kingdom, Mineral, Vegetable, and Animal, indeed for studying the triple subsistence in one created essence, in which he explored all virtues of the vegetable, animal, and mineral Nature.

Here the Paracelsian *tria prima* or three primaries (*drei Ersten*) correspond to the three kingdoms: mineral (salt), vegetal (mercury), and animal (sulphur); this fact is, we believe, not without deep implications for the laboratory alchemist. Three virtues, one nature. The epithet Trismegistos denotes at the same time the legendary father of all alchemists, and the Philosophical Mercury, which is thrice great as it rules over the three kingdoms of Nature.

In Paracelsus' writings, the *tria prima* are often compared to the three aspects that are present during the process of combustion (i.e. fire, smoke, ash): 'Whatever burns is sulphur, whatever is humid is mercury, and that which is the balsam of these two is salt'.[6] Paracelsians also employed the *tria prima* to represent the composition of the human microcosm: 'for Mercury is the spirit, Sulphur is the soul, and Salt is the body',[7] and this correlation was extended to

---

6   PARACELSUS, *Hermetic and Alchemical Writings*, ed., Waite, vol. I, pp. 258–59. As a historical note, it is important to recognise that the essential structure of the *tria prima* was already in place before Paracelsus (indeed, it is inherent to the composition of cinnabar—the salt [in a chemical sense] of sulphur and mercury). However, it is undeniable that the triad of sulphur, mercury, and salt was raised by Paracelsus to a previously unparalleled prominence. For the background to the alchemical meaning of salt before Paracelsus, see CHEAK, *Light Broken Through the Prism of Life*, pp. 36–42.

7   PARACELSUS, 'Concerning the Nature of Things', *Hermetic and Alchemical Writings*, ed., Waite. vol. I, p. 125.

the Christian trinity: father (sulphur), holy spirit (mercury), son (salt). 'In this manner', states Paracelsus, 'in three things, all has been created [...] namely, in salt, in sulphur, and in liquid [i.e. Mercury]. In these three things all things are contained, whether sensate or insensate [...] So too you understand that in the same manner that man is created [in the image of the triune God], so too all creatures are created in the number of the Trinity, in the number three'.[8]

Here and in the next two aphorisms, the virtues of the triple substance are further specified. Mercury gives the vegetating power (the power to grow), Sulphur the animating power (the power to ensoul), and finally Salt the persistence (the power to endure).

---

8   PARACELSUS, *Theologische und religionsphilosophische Schriften*, ed. Kurt Goldammer, Wiesbaden: Steiner, 1955, p. 63.

Canon 2

The vegetating force in the nature of the volatile Mercury lies in the likeness of a candid, concrete, uncommon snow, which is a certain Spirit of the major as well as the minor world, whence depends the mobility and fluidity of the same human nature, according to the rational soul.

The vegetating force is now described: it is said to be in the likeness of a pure or candid snow. We are reminded here of the tale of *Schneewittchen* (Snow White and the Seven Dwarves, from the Brothers Grimm): a rather clear allusion to the seven traditional metals and their common denominator, the common metallic mercury, which is white because it has been, as it were, 'washed' of its colours, i.e., its impure sulphurs.

In his *Le Triomphe hermétique ou la Pierre philosophale victorieuse* (The Hermetic Triumph or the Victorious Philosophical Stone, 1699), Limojon de Saint Didier (c. 1630–1689) says:

> *Vous ne trouverez plus de difficulté après cela, à conclure, que l'or métallique n'est pas celuy des Philosophes, et que ce n'est pas sans fondement, que dans la querelle dont il s'agît ici, la Pierre luy reproche, qu'il n'est pas tel, qu'il pense estre : mais que c'est elle, qui cache dans son sein le véritable Or des Sages, c'est à dire les deux premières sortes d'or, dont je viens de parler: car vous devez sçavoir que la Pierre estant la plus pure portion des Eléments métalliques, après la séparation, et la purification, que le Sage en a fait, il s'ensuit qu'elle est proprement l'or de la seconde espèce; mais lors que cet or parfaitement calciné, et exalté jusques à la netteté, et à la blancheur de la neige, a acquis par le magistère une sympathie naturelle avec l'or astral, dont*

il est visiblement devenu le véritable aimant, il attire, et il concentre en lui mesme une si grande quantité d'or astral, et de particules solaires, qu'il reçoit de l'émanation continuelle qui s'en fait du centre du Soleil, et de la Lune, qu'il se trouve dans la disposition prochaine d'estre l'Or vivant des Philosophes, infiniment plus noble, et plus précieux, que l'or métallique, qui est un corps sans âme, qui ne saurait estre vivifié, que par nôtre or vivant, et par le moyen de nostre Magistère.

You will not find any difficulty after this to conclude that metallic gold is not that of the philosophers, and that it is not without foundation that in the quarrel of which we are speaking here, the Stone reproaches him (metallic gold) for not being who he thinks he is, bur rather that it is she (the Stone) who hides in her breast the true Gold of the Wise, i.e., the first two kinds of gold of which I am going to speak. For you must know that the Stone is the purest part of the Metallic Elements, after the separation and purification performed by the Wise, and consequently that it is the gold of the second species. But when this perfectly calcined gold, exalted to the clear purity and the whiteness of snow, has acquired by the magistry a natural sympathy with the astral gold—for which it has visibly become the true magnet, attracting it, and concentrating within itself such a large quantity of astral gold and solar particles from the continual emanation that occurs from the centre of the Sun and the Moon—it subsequently finds itself in the [dis]position of being the living Gold of the Philosophers, infinitely nobler and more precious than metallic gold, which is simply a body without soul that can only be vivified by our living gold, by means of our Magistry.[9]

9   Amsterdam, H. Wetstein, 1699.

Limojon here is quite clear: the metallic gold can be calcined to a state which is like white snow. At that very point it becomes like a magnet for the astral gold, the solar particles (*particules*) which then 'charge' it with their power. Of course, one of the key problems in operative alchemy is: how to reduce metals to this candid snow? This text does not say anything about the secret procedure.

CANON 3

> *On the other hand, the animating force, as a glue of the World, is a medium between Spirit and body, and their reciprocal bond, without a doubt in the Sulphur of a certain reddish and transparent oil, like the Sun in the Major World and the heart of the Microcosm.*

The animating force holds together the body and the mercurial spirit. The chief function of sulphur (referring of course to the principle, not the common sulphur) is precisely this: to *coagulate* mercury, i.e., to *fix* it (lest it quickly leave the body).

Now, where is this precious sulphur? The canon gives us a precise hint: it is in a certain reddish oil. Oils, as a rule of thumb, are the vehicles of sulphur in every realm (for instance in the work on plants, the quintessence of a herb is to be found in its essential oil). Their importance cannot be underestimated. It is not by chance that oil was considered sacred in antiquity, and that the appointed king was anointed.

The red oil is described as the 'Sun in the Major World' (i.e., Macrocosm) and also as the 'heart of the Microcosm'. The same language—the 'Sun in the Macrocosm'—is used in Canon 18 to evoke the principle of *rubedo*: the great reddening that signifies the perfection of the alchemical Work, i.e., the attainment of the red tincture that transforms common bodies into divinely animated or philosophical bodies.

Thus, to reiterate, having looked at the trinitarian structure implicit in the figure of Hermes Trismegistus in canon one, the second canon descibes the vegetating power of mercury, and the third canon describes the animating power of sulphur. The next canon describes the alchemical salt.

Canon 4

Finally, minerality obtains a body in the guise of a Salt of remarkable virtue and smell, where salt from the earthly scoria shall be separated, not dissimilar to Mercury, except for the coarseness of the body and the consistency of the earth.

Here, the identification of salt with the body (*corpus*) in the microcosm and with the earth (*terra*) in the macrocosm is made more or less explicit. More specifically, however, the minerality (*mineralitas*), embodied in salt, described here as that which is separated from the 'earthly scoria' (*scoria terræ*), implies a wider alchemical principle: that of the alkaline salts that can be extracted from calcined mineral body.

The French Hermetic philosopher, René Schwaller de Lubicz (1887–1961), described salt as the immortal mineral remains which survive combustion and putrefaction. This salt was as both the 'foundation and support of the body' as well as the 'guardian of form'.[10] Just as mercury is the underlying fluid or informable substance, and sulphur is the informing principle, salt, or minerality, is that which *preserves* the form. This preserving function of salt is reiterated in canon six, which speaks of the 'consistency of salt which preserves from putrefaction' (*salis consistentia à putredine asservantis*).

This function is underscored by Paracelsus when he describes salt as 'the *balsam* of Nature, which drives away the corruption of the warm Sulphur [together] with the moist Mercury, out of which two components the human being is by nature compacted'.[11]

---

10 R. A. Schwaller de Lubicz, *Temple*, vol. 1, p. 67; André Vandenbroeck, *Al-Kemi*, p. 186.
11 Paracelsus, *The Economy of Minerals*, ch. 9: 'Concerning the

Some interesting hints may be added for the practicing alchemist: this salt, after the purification (which removes all unnecessary impurities from its perfect body), is said to be 'not dissimilar to Mercury'. Indeed, salt is just a coagulated version of mercury, so this is no surprise.

As a side note, in Daoist alchemy the *tria prima* are comparable to the *san bao* (三寶) or 'three treasures': *jing-qi-shen* (精氣神), which are comprised of 'esssence' (*jing*), 'vital energy' (*qi*), and 'spirit' (*shen*). Now *jing*, whose Chinese character is reminiscent of grain, is the equivalent of salt. When heated in the 'field of elixir' (*dan-tien*), it becomes *qi*, or mercury. (And here we must note that the term for 'elixir' in Chinese also means 'cinnabar', the salt of sulphur and mercury, or mercuric sulphide). Once again, this is a confirmation of the above: the three are, as the canons themselves tell us, three subsistences of one essence.

Virtues and Properties of Salts in Alchemy and in Medicine', in *Hermetic and Alchemical Writings*, ed. Waite, p. 98 (modified). Cf. our remarks on the *limbus* in the commentary to the next canon.

Canon 5

These three subsistences in one created essence constitute the limbus of the minor and major world, from which the first man was formed, having been shaped from the dust of the earth. Here enters the rational soul of the immortal Microcosm, immediately inspired by God, the moving and directing cause, like a Queen, of those three and all other functions.

Now that the three subsistences and their role has been made clear, this canon touches upon the substance itself, referred to as the *limbus*, following Paracelsus. But what exactly is this *limbus*?

According to Paracelsus, the first created things—heaven and earth—combine to form a *limbus*, a kind of 'prime matter' from which the first human being is created. In the Hebrew *Genesis*, this substance is identified with the earth (*adamah*) from which the first creature (*adam*) is formed: the substance into which God breathes his breath (*ruach*) in order to animate it.[12] Thus, the primordial living being is a juncture of three principles: heaven (spirit, mercurius), earth (substance, salt) and the animating soul (sulphur).

Linguistically speaking, the Latin term *limbus* evokes the *lima terræ* of the Vulgate *Genesis*: the 'slime of the earth' from which God fashioned Adam. However, the term itself more precisely refers to a border or edge, in particular the hem, girdle, or fringe of a garment. By extension it can also refer to any border-like fringe, and is possibly related to *limen*, 'threshold' or *limes*, 'limit'. Significantly, as 'girdle' it can refer to the belt of the zodiac (ecliptic), as well as the

---

12 Cf. the similar connection that pertains between Latin *humus*, 'earth, soil', and *humanus*, 'human'.

concentric celestial zones encircling the earth,[13] associations that soon become relevant in Paracelsian usage.

Beyond the explicit references to Judaic anthropogony, the core idea of the Paracelsian *limbus* is that man is not created from man, but from a pre-existing substance:

> *Nuhn ist der Mensch nicht auß dem Menschen geboren: Dann im ersten Menschen ist kein Vormensch gewesen/ sondern den Creatur/ vnd auß den* Creatis *ist der* Limbus/ *vnd der* Limbus *ist der Mensch worden/ vnd der Mensch is der* Limbus *bleiben.*

> The human being did not originate from the human being. For the first human being would have had no human precursor, but rather only [some created substance]; and out of the *creata* arose the *limbus*, and the *limbus* became the human being; and the human being has remained in the *limbus*.[14]

What is important to note here is that the Adamic matter is not merely 'earth' as we commonly conceive it, but an earth combined with or containing *celestial* essences. The *limbus* is the essential material of the invisible (celestial) and visible (earthly) human being, before the animating spirit is introduced.[15] Once again, what we see here is the conception of the primordial human entity as a juncture of sulphur (animating soul), mercury (vegetative spirit), and salt (earthly substance).

This understanding of the primordial human as a creature of both terrestrial and celestial provenance evokes a number of important mythological resonances. The 'true

---

13 WEEKS, *Paracelsus (Theophrastus Bombastus von Hohenheim, 1493–1541): Essential Theoretical Writings*, Leiden, Brill, 2007, p. 181 n. 2.
14 PARACELSUS, *Paragranum*, HUSER 2:49; trans, WEEKS, pp. 180/181.
15 WEEKS, *Paracelsus*, p. 180 n. a.

human being' (真人, *zhen ren*) of classical Daoism, for instance, is regarded as the perfect expression of 'heaven and earth',[16] while the Orphic gold lamellæ identify the initiate as 'a child of earth and starry heaven'.[17]

Examples could be multiplied, but it suffices to say that, because the human being is created from a substantial juncture of heaven and earth, its material composition is conceived as possessing an 'inner firmament', which forms the basis of the Paracelsian doctrine of macrocosmic and microcosmic astrological correspondences. 'The heavens operate within us' remarks Paracelsus,[18] and because of this, the true physician 'has the capacity to assess the heavens in the human being':

> *Dann so er den Himmel nur eusserlich weißt/ so bleibt er ein* Astronomus *vnd ein* Astrologus: *So ers aber im Menschen ordnet/ so weißt er zween Himmel.*

> For if he comprehends the heavens only in their external manifestation, he remains an *astronomus* and an *astrologus*. But as soon as he conceives the same within the human being, he is aware of two heavens.[19]

Ultimately, the Paracelsian theory of medicine follows from this: if a physician does not know the human being in its completeness, i.e. in its celestial and terrestrial nature,

---

16 Cf. *Huang Di neijing su wen,* 1-6-10, trans. UNSCHULD and TESSENOW, p. 42: 'They upheld [the patterns of] heaven and earth'.
17 See Fritz GRAF and Sara Iles JOHNSTON, eds., *Ritual Texts for the Afterlife: Orpheus and the Bacchic Gold Tablets,* New York: Routledge, 2007, pp. 5–7.
18 PARACELSUS, *Paragranum,* Huser 2:46; trans, Weeks, pp. 172/173: 'der Himmel in vns wirckt'.
19 PARACELSUS, *Paragranum,* Huser 2:47; trans, Weeks, pp. 174/175.

they will not know how to cure its illnesses. For human illnesses have a celestial as well as terrestrial origin, inherent in the *limbus*—the pre-ensouled juncture of heaven and earth. This double origin is reflected and preserved in the microcosm of the human being.

Canon 6

Moreover just as the vigour and life of our bodies is kept whole and sound due to the dust of the earth which has been coagulated from the four elements, and if the spirit of Mercury (the radical humidity), the sulphuric soul (the natural heat), together with the consistency of salt (which preserves from putrefaction) sweetly harmonise in one thing, then so vice versa: it is necessary to separate the immortal soul from the body of the conglobated dust of the earth, if in one or more of the three principles a defect is found. If this deficiency is in all principles, then death comes; if only in some, sickness ensues; which is mostly seen in the anatomy of the principal seven organs.

This canon reffirms the nature of the *tria prima* and specifies them further in the following way: mercury is 'spirit' (*spiritus*) but also 'radical humidity' (*humidum radicale*); sulphur is 'soul' (*anima*) but also 'natural heat' (*calidum naturale*); salt is 'body' (*corpus*) but also 'consistency' (*consiſtentia*) and 'preservation from putrefaction' (*à putredine aservantis*).

Insofar as it keeps the vitality of the body whole and sound, the 'dust of the earth' (*pulvere terræ*) is described in a similar way to salt. This dust is 'coagulated from the four elements' (*quatuor elementis*), which appears to suggest that each half of the primordial duality—heaven and earth—is itself subdivided into two parts. Heaven is comprised of the masculine elements, fire and air, while earth is comprised of the feminine elements, earth and water. These four elements thus combine as a pair—masculine heaven and feminine earth—to form the limbus or dust of the earth: the heaven-earth juncture which forms the *prima materia* of the microcosm.

This *limbus* is the primordial matter, of dual nature, coagulated in accordance with the *tria prima*. If these three principles are without blemish and well harmonised, health is maintained. If any of the principles have defects, sickness arises. When everything is out of sorts, death is the result. The canon concludes with a precious hint: look at the anatomy of the 'seven principal organs' (*septem principalium membrorum*). The Paracelsian doctrine of man as a microcosm containing celestial essences implies that the seven planets (along with their metallurgic equivalents, the seven metals), must have counterparts in the human body, as the following celebrated image from Georg Johann Gichtel's *Theosophia Practica* shows.[20]

On a philological level, it should be noted that when our text speaks of sulphur, mercury, and salt having the possibility to 'sweetly harmonise in one thing', it should be noted that the Latin term *conspirent*, which is correctly translated here in its proper sense, 'harmonise', unfortunately loses its literal meaning, 'breath together' (con-spire). This may prevent the reader from sensing the immediate allusion to the element air that is conveyed here, and also to the sense of life and animation (and thus the principle of sulphur) implied by breathing. The harmony of sulphur, mercury, and salt is a living, *breathing* entity. As we will see in our commentary to canon eight, it is only when God breathes the breath of life into the primordial man that Adam become a living soul.

---

20   GICHTEL was a disciple of Jakob BOEHME, who spread the Paracelsian gospel throughout reformed Europe

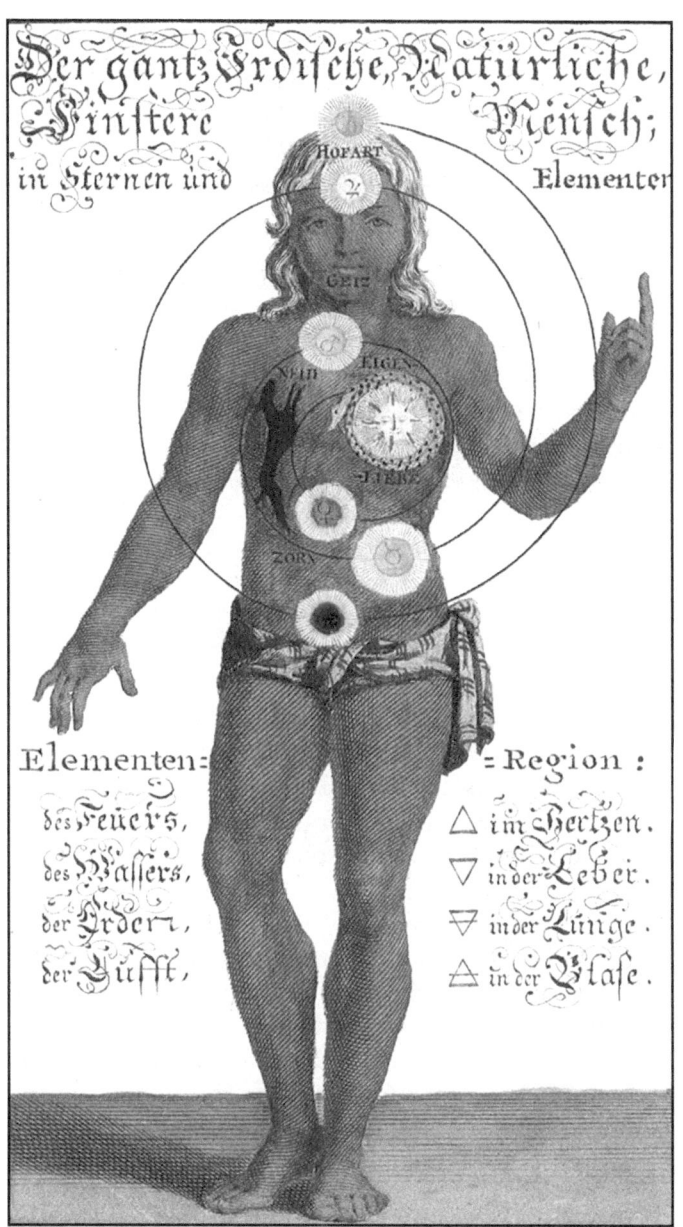

JOHANN GEORG GICHTEL, *Theosophia Practica*, 1722.

Canon 7

Nothing can remedy this triple defect as adequately as that mass of the limbus, conglobated from three principles into one, from which the first man was animated, which is exceedingly capable of rousing and nourishing the power and virtue of nature, if it will be duly turned in a fixed astral body.

In this canon the fundamental principle is established to maintain and recover health: just as the human being is formed fom the *limbus*, so too is the *limbus* itself coagulated from the *tria prima*, which is able to bring healing power back to nature. But to do so, it must be turned into a 'fixed astral body' (*corpus astrale fixum*). This is one of the chief secrets of alchemy: that the astral substance can be corporified, solidified into a concrete, tangible body. Then, and only then, can it be used to purge the body from all kinds of sickness.

The process of coagulation is of course but one half of a very old formula: the ability to spiritualise bodies and to corporealise spirits. In the words of Maria Prophetissa (first-to-third centuries): 'if you do not render corporeal substances incorporeal, and incorporeal substances corporeal, and if the two are not made one, nothing will be achieved'.[21] The seventeenth century Sufi, Muhzin Fayz Kāshānī, describes an equivalent process in which 'spirits are corporealised and bodies spiritualised', a process that, according to Henry Corbin, takes place in an ontologically real, yet liminal, zone—the *mundus imaginalis*—which Corbin defined precisely as a juncture between the eternal and the transient, the intelligible and the sensible: the *intermonde*

---

21 Marcellin BERTHELOT and C. E. RUELLE, *Collection des anciens alchimistes grecs*, Paris, Georges Steinheil, 1888–1889, vol. 2, §4.

or intermediary realm *par excellence*.[22]

In the alchemical purview, the 'higher' (heavenly) and 'lower' (earthly) aspects of existence are ultimately reciprocal and interdependent expressions of a deeper, more inclusive reality. Indeed, to separate alchemy into a purely material and a purely spiritual aspect in a mutually exclusive fashion, without recognising their fundamental complementarity, is to miss the greater flux between the volatile and the fixed with which alchemy is almost invariably concerned.

As a hieratic art, the alchemical vision of reality may be seen to encompass all levels of existence within a holarchical unity, and as such engages the world—including the world of duality subsumed in the greater whole—as a nondual reality (or to be more precise, a reality in which "two" exists in "one": a simultaneously abstract and concrete integrum). It is this 'conglobulated' reality that manifests in the substance of the *limbus*.

---

22   *Kalimāt maknūna* (Sayings Kept Secret), ch. xxx (Teheran, 1801), 68–70; (Bombay, 1296/1878), 69–72; trans. Henry CORBIN, *Spiritual Body and Celestial Earth*, p. 177.

Canon 8

> *From that can be understood that the Balsam of the Hermetic subject has a singular harmony with the human body: thence, that Swiss Monarch of the Physicians, Philip von Hohenheim alias Paracelsus, in the book on the Physical Stone, named The Manual, rightly affirms that this Medicine, not by opinion, but truly and properly, can, radically as something of the same kind, lead, preserve, and restore health to the Microcosm, which is located in the limbus of the Earth and was formed from the dust of earth.*

Whereas Paracelsian concepts have so far been implicit, this canon pays explicit homage to the Helvetic Monarch of Physicians himself: Philipus Theophrastus Bombastus von Hohenheim, alias Paracelsus. But what is of deeper interest here is the biblical reminder: man was formed from the *dust of the earth* (Genesis 2:7).

וייצר יהוה אלהים את־האדם עפר מן־האדמה ויפח באפיו
נשמת חיים ויהי האדם לנפש חיה:

And the LORD God formed man of the dust of the ground, and breathed into his nostrils the breath of life; and man became a living soul. (KJV)

Hebrew *aphar*, usually translated as 'dust' or 'dry earth', gives us another important clue to the *prima materia*. From dust we were made and to dust we return at the end of our mortal journey. The alchemist takes this as a sign that this dust forms the *limbus* of which the canons have already spoken.

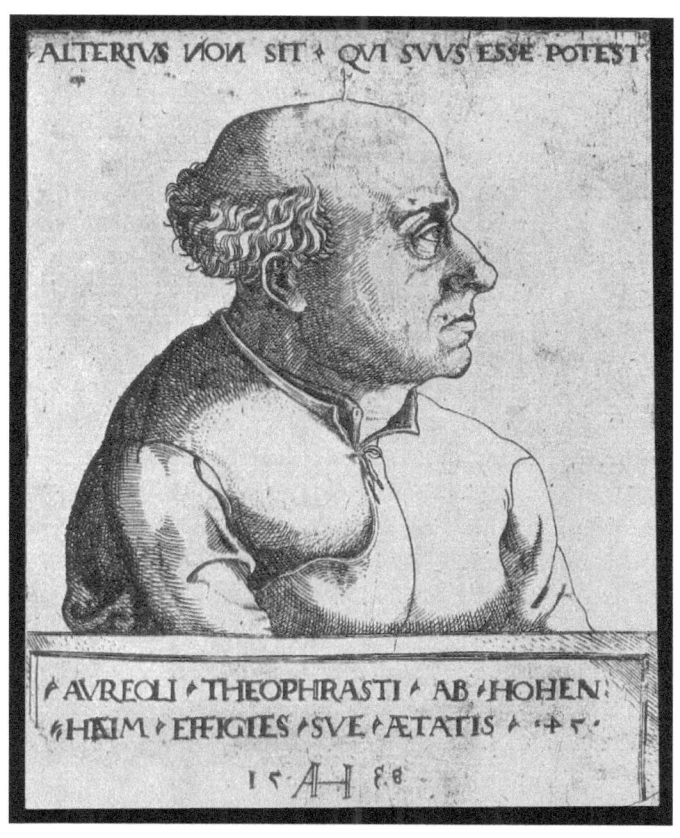

PHILIPUS THEOPHRASTUS BOMBASTUS
VON HOHENHEIM *alias* PARACELSUS
(1493/4–1541)

Etching by Augustin Hirschvogel, 1538

The nature of the Adamic matter, or the 'Philosophical Adam', is a theme with deep alchemical roots, stretching back as far as Zosimus of Panopolis, who taught that within the mortal body—the man of clay—there is an immortal fire, a man of light (*phōs*).[23] Indeed, whether conceived materially or spiritually, alchemy may to a large degree be defined by its concern to turn a mortal body into an immortal body. Or, stated differently, to extract or separate the incorruptible nature from the corruptible. The medical bases of alchemy are closely aligned with this, as are the conceptions of a primordial deathless *anthropos* from which we have fallen (and to which we may return).

'The Manual' of Paracelsus mentioned here most likely refers to *De Natura Rerum* (*Von den natürlichen Dingen*), 'On Natural Things', which in the manuscript version of the Bibliotheca Palatina is glossed as the *Manuale de lapide philosophico medicinali* (The Manual of the Medicinal Philosopher's Stone).[24]

23 See Howard M. JACKSON, ed., trans., *Zosimos of Panopolis, On the Letter Omega*, Society of Biblical Literature, Scholars Press, 1978.
24 Cod. Pal. germ. 295 Paracelsus: De natura rerum, dt. ; Manuale de lapide philosophico medicinali, dt. ; De praeparationibus, dt. u.a. ; Geber Latinus (?): De lapide philosophorum, dt., Universitätsbibliothek Heidelberg, 1573.

Canon 9

Truly, the greater the attention we pay to it, the weaker this common medicine is in radically keeping and directing the three principles of the microcosm and their reciprocal harmony: in fact (because it is almost wholly occupied with the four humours) it only helps give birth from the three principles indirectly.

The ninth canon recommends that we pay attention to this unique medicine, as ordinary medicaments only seldom embody the *tria prima*, only helping out with the four humours. As is well known, Paracelsus moved away from the traditional humoural medicine of late classical antiquity and the middle ages. Thus, this canon could be a slightly oblique, partisan reference to this paradigm shift.

On a philological level, it should be noted that the expression 'accidentally' (*ex accidenti*), which we have translated more loosely here as 'indirectly', should be taken in the Aristotelian sense, in which accidental properties (*per accidens, kata symbebekos*) are contrasted with essential properties (*per se, kath' hauto*). By implication, it is suggested that the four elements are accidental, while the three principles are essential.

Canon 10

Instead, the Mineral Chemical Medicine is rarely prepared and administered in the proper way from metals and minerals: hence Paracelsus in his book prefers his Medicine to all others. Nevertheless, he does not deny that great Arcana are inside other mineral things, but they require longer and more laborious work, and are not easily conquerable in a correct way, especially by amateurs; for when they come upon such matters, they often end up doing more harm than good.

Not only is the medicine proposed by Paracelsus declared to be the best, this canon seems to suggest that it is also the quickest to prepare. As such, we may be dealing with a more or less indirect hint at the so-called *via brevis*, the 'quick path', that some authors have advocated. Whereas many paths lead through rather tortuous tracks, the *via brevis* is the direct path to the stone of the wise.

Canon 11

Let us then search the Limbus of the Microcosm, in which it is situated; that is, that viscid globe of earth, made concrete from Mercury, Sulphur, and Salt: which because it comes into being from a certain humidity, can eloquently be called the viscid humidity of humidity, according to Geber.

Where is this *limbus* of the Microcosm? We must search for it in the microcosm itself, where it is situated. It takes the form of a viscid *globus* of earth that has been coagulated by the *tria prima*. This canon reminds us that, because it is generated by a certain humidity, it could be called the viscid humidity of humidity, a viscosisty coming out of humidity. That is what Geber, alias Al-Jabir, the great Arab alchemist, said about it. This appears to be cryptic. Where is this humidity from which we can collect the *limbus*? Let us continue to the next canon.

Canon 12

In fact, as the world has originated from Nothing, it owes its origin to Water, upon which the Spirit of the Lord lay: thence come forth all things, celestial and terrestrial alike. So, here emerges the Limbus from an uncommon Water, neither drawn from the celestial dew, nor from Air condensed in the caverns of the Earth, nor in the recipient itself, neither from the abyss of the Sea, nor from fountains, wells, or rivers, but from a certain Water over which we have laboured, which is ready at hand to everybody, but understood by very few. It possesses everything it needs for the completion of the entire work within itself, save for any external motion.

The twelfth canon refers back to the book of *Genesis*: the world, created out of nothing, owes its existence to a water from which everything was made. Now, this water, of paramount interest to the alchemist (because it is the primordial matter), is not common water. The canon stops short of any simple-minded search, not excluding the one that, in the wake of a verbatim reading of the *Mutus Liber*, identifies the dew spoken of by the alchemists with the common dew.

Yet, this water which is seemingly nowhere to be found is very well known, albeit only understood by the few. The attribute used by the canon to qualify this water is *perpessa*, i.e., the feminine perfect participle of the Latin verb *perpetior*, 'to endure'. It is a water which has endured sufferance. We shall not try to unravel the mystery of this *perpessa*; the reader is left with a topic for meditation.

Finally, this water is declared to have all that is needed, without a single 'kick' from outside. This is consonant with the celebrated alchemical *dictum*: one matter, one vessel, one operation.

Canon 13

Nevertheless, Nature is a certain medium between the Higher and Lower World, to be found everywhere, by both the poor and the rich alike, as all Philosophers attest. It is thrown into the streets, and trampled under feet, yet it is the fountain of admirable operations. Thence the three principia of our body, enjoying diverse properties, are to be restored.

This canon reiterates and expands upon the previous: this nature is midway between the two worlds, and can be found by everyone, as the chorus of ancient philosophers have repeated many times. We shall take no position here, but observe in passing that those who have taken human urine as their starting point do have some degree of support: after all, the text is explicit that the substance is thrown into the streets.

CANON 14

This matter, dissolved into its proper Water (for all generation comes forth from Water) is rotated across the four Elements, till it will be turned into a fixed Astral Matter, in a physical Egg, which is called so after the warmth of a Hen constantly incubating the egg. Else, all hope of birth would die.

Once acquired, the matter is dissolved in its own water because, as the canon reminds us, all generation comes forth from water. The rotation of the four elements is a circulation, repeated until it coagulates into a fixed astral matter (see aphorism 7). The image of the Hermetic Egg is topical: it indicates, among other things, the regime of fire to be adopted at this stage: a very mild heat, comparable to the one of the hen incubating her eggs (to produce this heat, alchemists used to put the vase under horse's manure).

The image of the egg in alchemical texts can be traced back to the *Greek Alchemical Corpus*, where it is indeed associated with the four elements. According to the 'Onomatopœia of the Egg' (*Onomatopoeiia tōu ōou*):

> It is said that the egg contains the four elements because it is the representation (*mimēsis*) of the cosmos, and that it encloses within itself the four elements; it is called the stone that moves the moon, the stone that is not a stone, the eagle stone, and the alabaster encephalon.[25]

25 BERTHELOT and RUELLE, *Collection des anciens alchimistes grecs*, vol. 1, §4.

Canon 15

Thus the Hermetic Bird once locked inside the Cave, which is the Oven, is to be roused gradually by the continuous heat of our vaporous fire, till it opens up and heals everything with its birth.

This canon reinforces the previous point: the heat to be employed at this stage is obtained from a vaporous fire. Little by little the bird absorbs the heat, until it is ready to emerge.

The Hermetic Bird or *Avis Hermetis* represents the liberation of the matter of the work. It is winged, because the divine Mercury is volatile; it is indeed a vapor, just like the etymology of Greek *pneuma*, Latin *spiritus*, or Chinese, *qi* (all of which point to a *breath* concept).

After liberating the bird from its cage, it is necessary to put it into a cave, which the text refers to as a *Furnus*, 'Oven' (cf. Italian *forno*, French *furneau*, English 'furnace'). This is true on many levels; to begin with it is to be taken literally, the bird is in an oven in which it can ripen. But there is more: it is also the dry earth that coagulates it, that keeps it protected and secured, all the while ensuring that the bird can receive nourishment and grow. Modern Hermetic philosophers such as René Schwaller de Lubicz would call this the *matrix* in which the volatile spirit of the metals can be brought back to life.[26] During this final phase of the magistry, traditionally known as the Third Opus, 'cooking' takes place by the sole agency of heat. This heat has to be administered judiciously, because too much or too little will kill the bird, exactly as with common eggs (hence the image of the egg in these canons). And so it naturally follows that

---

26 See R. A. SCHWALLER DE LUBICZ, *Notes et propos inédits*, 2 vols, Apremont: M.C.O.R/La Table d'Émeraude, 2006–2007.

the oven is also the Hermetic egg, a cosmic image with a rich symbolic history, as we have alluded to in our remarks upon the previous canon.

The third opus is easy, but it is also very secret. It has to do with the greatest secret of the opus, the *regime of fire*. In the end the oven/egg opens up—some texts seem to suggest that the physical container cracks—and the mature bird is released in its full glory. At that point all is done; the rest is multiplication (i.e., using the divine medicine to heal all that is imperfect, which is the topic of canon 18).

CANON 16

However, in the preparation of the three Principia of this troubled Water, we do not add to the substantial Matter, nor do we subtract anything from the three properties subsistent in it; we remove only the superfluous, namely the heterogeneous, like the dried Earth and the insipid water, so the Hermetic work is begun by the conjunction of the three Principles under a certain proportion, indeed with the weight of the body almost equal to the sesquialter part of spirit and soul.

This canon insists on the fact that this water has all that is needed. The work simply gets rid of superflous matters. After all the dross has been removed and the three principles have been separated (in other words, the *solve* is complete), we need to put them back together, but in a specfic proportion: the weight of the salt is to be 3/2 of the Mercury and Sulphur combined.

The term sesquialter (or sesquialtera), it should be noted, is an obscure English word derived from the Latin term for a proportion of one and a half. More precisely, it refers to the ratio 3:2, and in musical harmony, refers to the *hemiola*, or perfect fifth. The topic of harmonic proportions in alchemical compositions hints at a deeper philosophy of measure underpinning Hermetic precept and practice, which remains to be investigated in more detail by future researchers. The obvious point of departure in this regard is Schwaller de Lubicz's work on the principles of harmony employed in Egyptian art in general, and in the divine temple in particular.[27]

---

27   See R. A. SCHWALLER DE LUBICZ, *Le Temple de l'homme : Apet du sud à Louqsor*. 3 vols. Paris, Caractère, 1957.

Canon 17

Afterwards all things have to be regulated by a continuous heat, so that the Agent inside Nature neither stops, nor suffers an excess. Let there be a mild fire in the beginning, initially of 4 drops or threads, till the Matter becomes black. Then add almost 14 threads till it washes itself, and the appearing Iris ends in a Grey colour. Then persevere with almost 24 threads, till a perfect Albedo [appears], superior to Snow, fluid and fixed, which is the Moon of the Microcosm.

We were not able to discover what kind of measure a thread is. Yet the numerics involved are of interest: four, then fourteen, then twenty-four, as the matter progresses to the perfect black (*nigredo*), then to the Iris of colours until grey, until finally it reaches the pristine white (*albedo*), where it becomes the philosophical moon (i.e., silver).

Iris refers to the Greek goddess of the rainbow, and thus to the spectrum of colour. The word for rainbow in Greek is *irin tēn ouranian*, 'the iris of the heavens'. However, the word *iris* is glossed in the Liddell-Scott-Jones lexicon as 'any bright-coloured circle surrounding another body' such as the 'lunar rainbow', the 'halo' surrounding a candle or the 'eyes' of a peacock's tail, as well as the 'iris of the eye'.[28] In alchemical contexts, this appearance of colour is usually referred to as the 'peacock's tail' (*cauda pavonis*), but the symbol of the iris is also used, and has a deeper significance. The iris appears *between* the perfect black of the pupil and the pristine white body of the eye. Similarly, our text tells us that the iris appears *between* the *nigredo* and the *albedo*.

28 LIDDELL, Henry George, and Robert SCOTT. *A Greek-English Lexicon, Revised and Augmented throughout by Sir Henry Stuart Jones, with the assistance of Roderick McKenzie.* Oxford, Clarendon Press, 1940, *vide: iris.*

We may point to some resonances here with Goethean colour theory, in which the colour phenomenon occurs on the border of darkness and light (in contrast to Newtonian theory, which holds that coloured light was a decomposition of white light alone).

These alchemical associations of the iris and pupil, and the coloured threshold between black and white, have their roots in the Greek and Egyptian origins of alchemy. Olympiodorus, citing Zosimos, remarks:

> There are two pure colours: white and black. White is expansive and dilating (*diakritikon*), black contractive and densifying (*synektikon*). Zosimos, alluding to nature, says: 'the pupil of the eye (*korēn tou ophthalmou*) is surrounded by the rainbow, or the iris of the heavens' (*irin tēn ouranian*). The ignorant do not realise that this is simply the expansive and contractive.[29]

---

29 OLYMPIODORUS, 'On the Sacred Art', in BERTHELOT and RUELLE, *Collection des anciens alchimistes grecs*, vol. 2, § 4.39. See further discussion in CHEAK, 'The Perfect Black: Egypt and Alchemy', in *Alchemical Traditions: From Antiquity to the Avant-Garde*, ed. CHEAK, revised ed., Auckland, Rubedo Press, 2018.

Canon 18

Thus, if you wish to proceed to the perfect Rubedo, you will maintain your fire for 70 days, till the Stone will be turned into a translucent Ruby of great weight, which is indeed the Sun of the Microcosm, to be augmented in the same way as when it was begun. A grain of this is equivalent to six-thousand grains, and is therefore to be administered in a very small dose.

The real difficulty of the work, and also the real secret, is to procure the initial water (the so-called first operation), and to obtain the separated principles. Afterwards, they must be recombined. The rest of the work is fairly straightforward: the progressive regime of fire perfects the stone. The end result is the manifestation of the 'Sun of the Microcosm' (*Sol Microcosmi*) in the form of a 'translucent ruby' (*Rubinum pellucidum*). The medicine has now crystallised into its most potent state, and it can be used sparingly.

Radix Elixiris

Root of the Elixir. Δ. R. E. I.
The vigor and the celestial image is inspired of that
one, whence flows this medicine of God.

The final rubric which seals the *Basilian Aphorisms* is the *Radix Elixiris*, or 'Root of the Elixir'. Here we are presented with a formulation composed of a triangle and the letters R.E.I. Ostensibly, what we have here is simply the initials of Raphæl Eglinus Iconius surmounted by a triangle. However, two other layers of meaning are also possible.

Firstly, reading the triangle as a Greek *delta* (Δ = 'D') gives us the German word *drei*, 'three': (D)REI. In the original German of Paracelsus, the *tria prima* are referred to as the *drei Ersten*, literally the 'three firsts', which equates to the Latin *tria prima*, 'three primaries'.

Secondly, given that the text was composed in Latin, we can read it simply as a triangle at the summit of the word *rei*, i.e., the genitive form of the word *rēs*, 'thing'. (The alchemical Rebis, for example, is literally the 'binary thing', or *rēs bina*). We must remember, however, that the ultimate meaning of *rēs* is not merely 'thing', but the very idea of what is 'real' (actually existing).

Whatever interpretation we favour, the rubric is indicating the triangular nature of reality, or the triadic wholeness of the three kingdoms, which are the *root of the elixir*, because the matter that the alchemist works with is not merely a material body, but an animated, ensouled body, formed of the three primaries, sulphur, mercury, and salt.

In short, alchemy is not simply a manipulaton of matter through chemical processes of separation and synthesis; rather, it demands a philosophy of nature, a theology of material reality (*rēs*), in which the animating and vegetative processes, which unfold through nature, can be comprehended as a triadic yet integral whole.

Finally, in regards to the 'medicine of God' (*medicina Dei*), it may be noted that the stone is often called *Donum Dei*, or 'Gift of God'.[30] In Christian symbology, one could say that Christ is the stone in the human sphere, but it would be equally correct to say that the mineral stone is like the Christic son in its own domain. Or even more broadly, one could say that each domain has its own completion, its inner perfection, and that the path to bring about such a perfection is essentially the same.

---

30 See the 'Preface' to FULCANELLI, *Le Mystère des cathédrales et l'interprétation ésotérique des symboles hermétiques du grand œuvre*. Paris, Jean Schmidt, 1926.

Bibliography

Anon. *Mutus Liber.* Pierre Savouret, La Rochelle, 1677.

Berthelot, Marcellin, and C. E. Ruelle. *Collection des anciens alchimistes grecs.* 3 vols. Paris, Georges Steinheil, 1888–1889.

Böke, Christer, Koopmans, John, Klossowski de Rola, Stanislas, and Aaron Cheak, eds., trans. *Hermetic Recreations: Including the Scholium.* Auckland, Rubedo Press, 2018.

Bruno, Giordano. *Summa Terminorum metaphysicorum ad capessendum Logicæ et Philosophiæ studium, ex Iordani Bruni Nolani Entis descensu manusc. excerpta; nunc primum luci commissa; a Rephæle Eglino leonio, Tigurino.* Tiguri, apud Ioannem Wolphium, 1595.

Cheak, Aaron. *Light Broken Through the Prism of Life: René Schwaller de Lubicz and the Hermetic Problem of Salt.* Dissertation, University of Queensland, 2011.

———. ed. *Alchemical Traditions: From Antiquity to the Avant-Garde,* 2013; revised edition, Auckland, Rubedo Press, 2018 (forthcoming).

———. 'The Perfect Black: Egypt and Alchemy', in *Alchemical Traditions: From Antiquity to the Avant-Garde,* edited by Aaron Cheak, 2013; revised edition, Auckland, Rubedo Press, 2018.

Colunga, Alberto, and Laurentio Turrado, eds. *Biblia Sacra, iuxta Vulgatum Clementinam. Nova Editio.* Fifth Edition. Madrid, Biblioteca de Autores Cristianos, 1977.

Copenhaver, Brian P., ed., trans. *Hermetica: The Greek Corpus Hermeticum and the Latin Asclepius in a new English Transla-*

tion. Cambridge, Cambridge University Press, 2002.

CORBIN, Henry. *Spiritual Body and Celestial Earth: From Mazdean Iran to Shī'ite Iran*. Trans. Nancy PEARSON. Princeton, Princeton University Press, 1977.

DEBUS, Allen G. 'Basil Valentine', in *Dictionary of Scientific Biography*, vol. 13, pp. 94 ff. New York, Scribner's, 1976.

_____. *The Chemical Philosophy: Paracelsian Science and Medicine in the Sixteenth and Seventeenth Centuries*. New York, Science History Publications, 1976.

DORN, Gerhardus. *De transmutatione metallorum*, in Lazarus ZETZNER, Lazarus, ed., *Theatrum Chemicum*, vol. I, Strasbourg, 1602.

EGLINUS, Raphæl. *Cheiragogia Heliana de Auro Philosophico necdum cognito; unde juxta facile percipi potest tum opus universalissimum totius Monarchiæ Chymicæ in regno minerali; tum omnes in suo quin genere universales ejusdem regni mineralis lapides, tincturæve particulares, cujus author, N. Niger Hapelius, anagrammatizomenos*. Marburg, Rudolph Hutwelcher, 1612.

_____. *Disquisitio de Helia Artista, in qua de metallorum transformatione adversus Hagelii et Pererii Jesuitarum opiniones, evidenter et solide disseritur. Editio postrema correctior et melior. Accesserunt recens Canones Hermetici de Spiritu, Anima et Corpore majoris et minoris Mundi, cum appendice*. Marpurgi, Typis Hutwelckerianis, 1608.

FAIVRE, Anoine. 'Elie Artiste, ou le messie des philosophes de la nature (première partie)', *Aries* 2.2 (2002), pp. 119–152.

FERGUSON, John. *Bibliotheca Chemica*. 1906; reprint, 1954, volume I, pp. 232–33.

FULCANELLI. *Le Mystère des cathédrales et l'interprétation ésotérique des symboles hermétiques du grand œuvre*. Paris, Jean Schmidt, 1926.

GICHTEL, Johann Georg. *Theosophia Practica: Halten und Kämpfen ob dem H. Glauben bis ans Ende: durch die drey Alter des Lebens Jesu Christi, nach den dreyen Principien Göttliches-Wes-*

ens, mit derselben Ein- und Aus-Gebuhrt durch Sophiam in der Menschheit, welche Gott derselben in diesem Alter der Zeit von neuem vermählet hat: und gute und böse Menschen, kluge und töhrichte Jungfrauen zu der grossen Hochzeit des Lamms eingeladen: auf dass eine jede Seele, wie verdorben sie auch immer sey, sich mit diesem lieblichen Evangelio erwecken und ihren Willen mit Gottes Willen vereinigen möge zu solcher göttlichen Eheligung: und so dan mit diesem göttlichen Wort in christo sich schwängern, und aus der bösen sundlichen Natur in ihre erste göttliche Bildniss sich wiederum eingebären möge durch Jesum: auf Veranlassung in Briefen gestellet von dem gottseligen Gottes-Freund und Mann Sophiae. Leyden, 1722.

GEO. THOR. ASTROMAGUS. *Cheiragogia heliana: A manuduction to the philosopher's magical gold: out of which profound, and subtile discourse; two of the particullar tinctures, that of Saturn and Jupiter conflate; and of Jupiter single, are recommended as short and profitable works, by the restorer of it to the light. To which is added; Antron Mitras; Zoroaster's cave: or, An intellectuall echo, &c. Together with the famous Catholic epistle of John Pontanus upon the minerall fire.* London, Humphrey Moseley, 1659.

KOPP, Hermann. *Beiträge zur Geschichte der Chemie.* Braunschweig, Vieweg, 1869–1875.

GÖRMAR, Gerhard. 'Johann Thölde, Herausgeber der Schriften des „Basilius Valentinus" und Verfasser der *Haliographia*— eine biographische Skizze', *Mitteilung (Gesellschaft Deutscher Chemiker)* 16, 2002, pp. 3–19.

GRAF, Fritz, and Sara Iles JOHNSTON, eds. *Ritual Texts for the Afterlife: Orpheus and the Bacchic Gold Tablets.* New York: Routledge, 2007.

HAGELIUS, Balthasar. *Disputatio philosophica de metallo et lapide: ex tertio et quarto libro meteororum Aristotelis.* Ingolstadii, Sartorius, 1588.

IVERSEN, Erik. *Egyptian and Hermetic Doctrine.* Copenhagen, Museum Tusculanum Press, 1984.

JACKSON, Howard M., ed., trans. *Zosimos of Panopolis, On the*

Letter Omega, Society of Biblical Literature, Scholars Press, 1978.

KOPP, Hermann. *Beiträge zur Geschichte der Chemie*. Braunschweig, 1869–1875.

LIDDELL, Henry George, and Robert SCOTT. *A Greek-English Lexicon, Revised and Augmented throughout by Sir Henry Stuart Jones, with the assistance of Roderick McKenzie*. Oxford, Clarendon Press, 1940.

LIMOJON DE SAINT DIDIER, Alexandre-Toussaint. *Le Triomphe hermétique ou la Pierre philosophale victorieuse*. Amsterdam, Henry Wetstein, 1699.

MARRA, Massimo, ed., and Michela BRINDISI, trans. 'Gli aforismi basiliani di Eglinus Iconius (Angelus Medicus). Simbolismo ermetico e influenze paracelsiane in un testo alchemico seicentesco', *Abstracta*. www.massimomarra.net

MORAN, Bruce T. 'Alchemy, Prophecy, and the Rosicrucians: Raphæl Eglinus and Mystical Currents of the Early Seventeenth Century', in P. RATTANSI and A. CLERICUZIO, eds., *Alchemy and Chemistry in the 16th and 17th Centuries*, pp. 103-119. Dordrecht, Springer, 1994.

MOTSCHMANN, J. Ch., *Erfordia Literata*. Erfurt, 1729.

NEMO, C., and F. CERCONE. *Philalethe Reveal'd, vol. 2*. Nautilus Editions & Alla Via Jacobea Editions, 2016.

NOCK, Arthur Darby, and A. J. FESTUGIÈRE, eds, trans. *Corpus Hermeticum*. Paris, Les Belles lettres, 1945.

PAGEL, Walter. *Paracelsus: An Introduction to Philosophical Medicine in the Era of the Renaissance*. Basel, Karger, 1958.

PARACELSUS (Theophrastus Bombastus von Hohenheim). *Cod. Pal. germ. 295 Paracelsus: De natura rerum, dt. ; Manuale de lapide philosophico medicinali, dt. ; De praeparationibus, dt. u.a. ; Geber Latinus (?): De lapide philosophorum, dt.* Universitätsbibliothek Heidelberg, 1573.

———. *Opera Bücher vnd Schrifften*. Edited by Johannes HUSER,

Basel, Konrad Waldkirch, 1589–1591.

———. *The Hermetic and Alchemical Writings of Paracelsus.* Edited by Arthur E. WAITE. London, J. Elliott & Co., 1894.

———. *Sämtliche Werke.* Edited by Karl SUDHOFF. München, R. Oldenbourg, 1929–1933.

———. *Theologische und religionsphilosophische Schriften*, ed. Kurt GOLDAMMER. Wiesbaden, Steiner, 1955.

———. *Paracelsus (Theophrastus Bombastus von Hohenheim, 1493–1541): Essential Theoretical Writings.* Edited and translated by Andrew WEEKS. Leiden, Brill, 2007.

PLATO. *Complete Works.* Ed. John M. Cooper. Indianapolis, Hackett, 2009.

RATTANSI , P., and A. CLERICUZIO, eds. *Alchemy and Chemistry in the 16th and 17th Centuries.* Dordrecht, Springer, 1994.

SALAMAN, Clement, Dorine VAN OYEN, William D. WHARTON, and Jean-Pierre MAHÉ, eds., trans. *The Way of Hermes: The Corpus Hermeticum.* London, Duckworth, 2004.

SCOTT, Walter, ed., trans. *Hermetica: The Ancient Greek and Latin Writings which contain Religious or Philosophic Teachings ascribed to Hermes Trismegistus.* Shambhala, 1985.

SCHWALLER DE LUBICZ, R. A. *Le Temple de l'homme : Apet du sud à Louqsor.* 3 vols. Paris, Caractère, 1957.

———. *Notes et propos inédits.* 2 vols. Apremont: M.C.O.R/La Table d'Émeraude, 2006–2007.

SUCHTEN, Alexander von. *De secretis antimonii.* Strassburg, Ch. Müllers Erben, 1570.

THÖLDE, Johann. *Haligraphia, das ist, Gründliche und eigendliche Beschreibung aller Saltz Mineralien : Darin von deß Saltzes erster Materia, Ursprung, Geschlecht, Unterscheid, Eigenschafft ... gehandelt wird ; Beneben einer Historischen Beschreibung aller Saltzwercke ... ; Auch wie man aus allen Metallen und vornembsten Mineralien ... ihre Saltz außziehen, und zu Menschlicher Gesundheit brauchen sol.* Leipzig, Apel, 1603.

UNSCHULD, Paul U., and Hermann TESSENOW. *Huang Di neijing su wen: An Annotated Translation of Huang Di's Inner Classic—Basic Questions*. Berkeley, University of California Press, 2011.

UŽDAVINYS, Algis. *Philosophy as a Rite of Rebirth: From Ancient Egypt to Neoplatonism*. Wiltshire, Prometheus Trust, 2008.

VALENTINUS, Basilius. *Ein kurtz summarischer Tractat, von dem grossen Stein der Uralten*. Eisleben, Bartholomaeus Hornigk, 1599.

———. *Triumph Wagen Antimonii*. Leipzig, Jakob Apel, 1604.

———. *De Microcosmo: Deque magno mundi mysterio et medicina hominis liber geminus, Magni Basilii Valentini, quondam ordinis benedictini philosophi germani: Exterorum in gratiam recens, ab Angelo Medico latinitate donatus, cum interpretis aphorismis Basilianis et præfatione philosophica, to Illustriss. Celsissimumque Principem Dn. Augustum Anhaltinum &c*. Marpurgi, Typis Guolgangi Kezelii, 1609.

———. *De Microcosmo, oder von den kleinen Welt des menschlichen Leibes, Fr. Basili Valentini, Benedictiner Ordens, was solche in sich hält, woraus sie zusammen gebaut, und was ihr ganzer Begriff und Inhalt vermag, sammt ihrem Ende und Ausgang, allen so den Grund der Weisheit lieben, das Vornehmst, und zu wissen höchlich vonnöthen*. In *Chymische Schriften*, pp. 103–118. Hamburg, 1677.

———. *Chymische Schriften*. Hamburg, 1677.

VANDENBROECK, André. *Al-Kemi: Hermetic, Occult, Political, and Private Aspects of R. A. Schwaller de Lubicz*. Inner Traditions/Lindisfarne Press Uroboros Series v. 1. Rochester, Vermont, Lindisfarne Press, 1987.

WATANABE-O'KELLY, H. *Court Culture in Dresden*. London, Palgrave Macmillan, 2002.

ZETZNER, Lazarus, ed. *Theatrum Chemicum, præcipuos selectorum auctorum tractatus de Chemiæ et Lapidis Philosophici Antiquitate, veritate, jure præstantia, et operationibus continens in gra-*

tiam veræ Chemiæ et Medicinæ Chemicæ Studiosorum (ut qui uberrimam unde optimorum remediorum messem facere poterunt) congestum et in quatuor partes seu volumina digestum. 6 volumes. Oberursel and Strasbourg, Argentorati, Sumptibus heredum E. Zetzneri, 1602–1661.

ABOUT THE EDITORS

MIRCO A. MANNUCCI (PhD, City University of New York), is, in his own neologism, a holomath, i.e., that special breed of polymath who ceaselessly strives to link the tangled threads of his multifarious interests into an compact whole. A mathematician, a writer, an inveterate traveler, a practitioner of internal and external alchemy, a *Waldgänger*, a social media entrepreneur, an ascetic hedonist, he has rejected the artificial borders of so-called education to reach that twilight zone where the Great Work begins. Dr. Mannucci is the co-author of a Cambridge University Press book on quantum computing, has written a collection of Hermetic poems soon to be released through Rubedo Press, and is currently working on a philosophical science fiction novel. Last but not least, he is the co-founder of GaldraTek Corporation, which is focused on Augmented Social Reality.

AARON CHEAK (PhD, University of Queensland) is a scholar of comparative religion, philosophy, and esotericism. Straddling the interstices between integral and Hermetic philosophy, he received his doctorate in 2011 for his thesis on René Schwaller de Lubicz, and served as president of the international Jean Gebser Society from 2013–2015. He has appeared in a range of academic and esoteric publications, including *Light Broken through the Prism of Life* (2011), *Diaphany* (2015), and *The Leaf of Immortality* (2017). He currently directs Rubedo Press from the west coast of New Zealand, where he maintains an active interest in tea, wine, poetry, typography, and alchemy.

www.ingramcontent.com/pod-product-compliance
Lightning Source LLC
Chambersburg PA
CBHW021956290426
44108CB00012B/1098